# Portrait Quilts
## Painted Faces You Can Do

by

Bonnie Lyn McCaffery

## Credits

### Editors
Carly Jean Longhenry
Heather Lyn Radomsky

### Book Design/Illustration
Bonnie Lyn McCaffery

### Photography
Michael McCaffery

Portrait Quilts: Painted Faces You Can Do
©2005 by Bonnie Lyn McCaffery

Dream Mountain Studios
HC-8 Box 8526
Hawley, PA 18428 USA

Printed in USA

No part of this product may be reproduced in any form, unless otherwise stated, in which case reproduction is limited to the use of the purchaser. The written instructions, photographs, designs, projects, and patterns are intended for the personal, noncommercial use of the retail purchaser and are under federal copyright laws; they are not to be reproduced by any electronic, mechanical, or other means, including informational storage or retrieval systems, for commercial use.

The information in this book is presented in good faith, but no warranty is given nor results guaranteed. Dream Mountain Studios has no control over choice of materials or procedures and the company assumes no responsibility for the use of this information.

McCaffery, Bonnie Lyn,
Portrait Quilts: Painted Faces You Can Do
p. cm.
Includes bibliographical references.
ISBN 0-9766934-3-7

## Dedication

I am blessed with a terrific family. I have three daughters, Heather, Carly, and Abby, who are fine young woman on their own. My husband, Michael, is the amazing man who stands by my side and encourages me onward. I thank each of them for their support on this project. Carly shares her face to be painted by the hundreds of students who take the "Painted Face" class. Thank you to Heather and Carly for their help in editing this book. Michael did the photography and behind the scenes work on the book.

Thank you so much for your encouragement and support.

## Acknowledgements

Thank you to all of the generous people who loaned quilts to be included in the book: Deirdre Abbotts, Barbara Anderson, Diann E. Becker, Sandra J. Brenzel, Marie B. DiGerlando, JoAnne M. Finnigan, B. J. Herter, Carol A. Hill, Maureen Forseth, Kathleen J. Isaacks, Kathy Krause, Helen P. Marinaro, Mary P. Murray, Kathy Oehlmann, Lynn Page, Marion Poplawski, Kathleen Porycki, Linda Shorten, Barbara Staskowski, and Michelle Verbeeck.

Thank you to Judy Brumbaugh for her help with editing.

Thank you to the members of the Milford Valley Quilters Guild who continue to support me in my ventures into creative techniques and their willingness to act as my testing lab for workshops.

I would like to thank the following companies for their generous support: Bernina of America; Creative Crystal Company; DecoArt Inc.; Expo International Inc.; Hoffman California Fabrics; Robert Kaufman Company; Loew-Cornell; YLI Corporation; and Z-Barten Productions.

# Table of Contents

## SECTION I Get Ready
Supplies     7
- Fabrics
- Paint supplies
- Art Supplies
- Sewing Supplies
- Tools

Preparation     13
- Photographs and guideline drawing preparation

## SECTION II Let's Paint
Shading the Face     17
- Painting the Face
- Shading

Lips     23

Nose & Eye Shading     25
- Nose
- Additional Shading in the Eye Area

Eyes     27
- Painting the Iris
- Painting the Whites of the Eyes
- Eyebrows
- Eyelashes & Eyeliner
- Highlights

Freckles, Wrinkles, & Moles     33

Teeth     35

Painting Men & Children     39
- Men's Faces
- Children's Faces

Eyeglasses     41

Painting Other Items     43
- Hands and Feet
- Clothing

## SECTION III Designing the Portrait
Backgrounds     45
- Lining the face
- Background

Clothing     51
- Clothing
- Creative Clothing Ideas

Hair     57
- Hair
- Creative Hair Ideas

Creative Possibilities     65
- Sepia Tone Portraits
- Miniatures
- Photo Transfers
- Captured Items – The "Fantasy Fabric" Way

## SECTION IV Finishing the Portrait
Layering & Stitching     73
- Tulle Top Layer
- Pinning the Layers
- Stitching
- Trimming the Tulle
- Appliquéd Edges

Borders & Frames     77
- Simple Borders
- Easy Accent Borders
- Couched Accent Border
- Crazy Patch Borders
- Decorative Stitched Borders
- Photo Transfers
- Oval Borders

Finishing Touches     83
- Quilting
- Embellishments
- Binding and Labeling

## SECTION V Basic Steps
Quick Review     87
- Basic Step-by-Step Procedure

Resources & Bibliography     95

About the Author     96

**Contemplation III: Oh Just To Be** by Bonnie Lyn McCaffery, 2002, Hawley, PA, 44" x 50". Twisted branches on the sides of her are made from ribbon and fabric twisted to create realistic looking branches. Artificial flowers and leaves are captured under the tulle. Iridescent cellophane adorns her wings. Tintzl and Creative Crystal Rhinestones sparkle in the sky.

# Introduction

Many quilts that I have made with a person in it have sold soon after they were made. What an interesting thought! We find designs with people in them much easier to relate to. We can imagine the thoughts and feelings of the person in the quilt. We all love faces and if you're reading this book, you probably love fabric too. So why not combine these two loves and create a quilt with a face in it?

In my earlier quilts, when I wanted to include a person, I left out all of the facial details. This way I would not have to worry about getting everything perfect. I eventually attempted some very basic faces. This was better, but I knew there was still room to improve.

I wanted to be able to teach this, so I had to find a way that would make it very doable. I found that if I made a tracing of the face, then I would know exactly where each of the facial features belonged. This took much of the guesswork out of the process. I placed the tracing under the fabric in order to have a reference for painting the features.

A couple of face quilts later, I was off and running with a great way to be able to create painted faces that could be used in quilts.

I would recommend that you read through the book to get a general idea of how the technique works. Then follow the step-by-step instructions to paint the "Basic Beauty". This will give you confidence that YES! you can do this. Believe me, you really can do this. Give it a try and I think you will be amazed with your results.

Once you have painted the "Basic Beauty," you will be able to give her a personality all your own by the choice of hair and clothing. Go ahead and make her into a quilt following the instructions in the book. You will then be ready to create a painted face quilt of a person of your choice.

We'll explore several possibilities for backgrounds and borders. Once you start thinking creatively, you will come up with lots of great ideas to complete your painted face quilts.

Have fun and repeat after me…"I can do this."

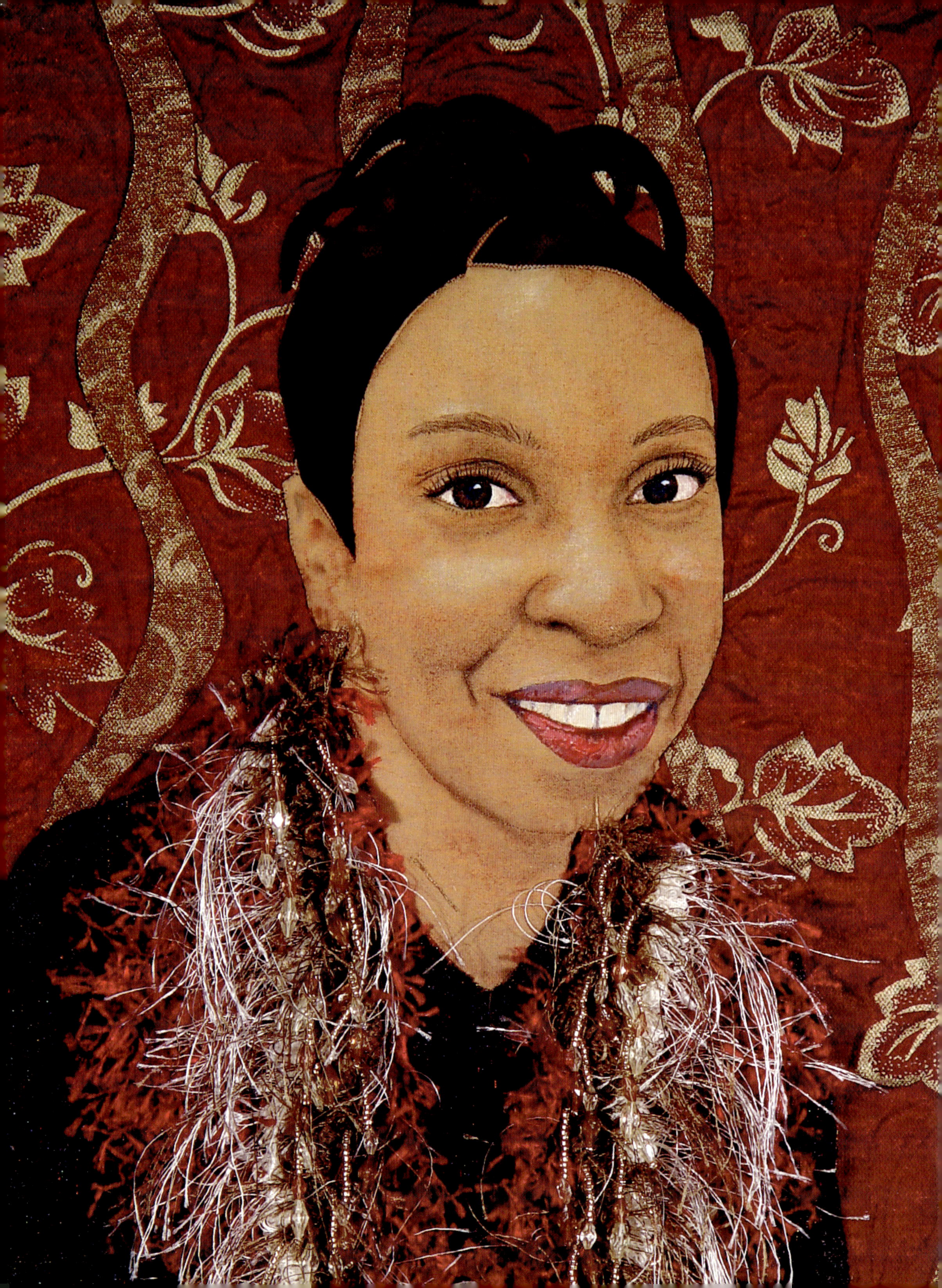

# SECTION I: Get Ready
## Supplies

The supplies you need are a combination of art supplies and sewing supplies.

### Fabrics
The face, hair, clothing, background, and borders are all made from fabric.

### Flesh
100% cotton is the best choice for any pieces that will be painted. Flesh colored fabric is needed for the face and any other area of flesh that is showing. It is amazing how many different colors of flesh there are. Some people have a peach, yellow, pink, tan, or brown tone. A good way to choose the flesh fabric is to take your photo to the fabric store and search for a color similar to the light to medium colored areas of the flesh. People are not usually pink, so take care to select something that is more flesh colored. Robert Kaufman Kona® Cotton Solids have a wonderful selection of solid colored cottons.

If all you can find is a pale pink, it is very easy to alter the shade to flesh tone by tea dyeing it.

### Hair
You have the option to create hair color similar to the photograph or you may chose to be creative and give your face a different color and style of hair. Look carefully at some photographs of hair. You will notice that there are highlights and shadows. Sometimes hair will reflect some of the colors around it. Notice the variety of colors in the hair in "Autumn" on page 32. Try to look carefully at these isolated colors. These will be the colors of fabric you will look for in the hair fabric. Don't be afraid to add some tiny highlight colors other than human color hair.

Cotton is a good choice for hair, but don't hesitate to look at other types of fabric as well. Organza, sparkly sheers, soft suede cloths, and just about any other type of fabric can be incorporated into the hair.

When looking at the color of the cotton fabrics for hair, be sure to look at both sides of the fabric. The fabric can be cut and flipped to the back side. Fabrics with a curvy or swirling texture might be the perfect texture of hair. I also like the subtle shading of Robert Kaufman Fabrics Kona® Multi-Dye fabrics. These will add realistic shadows and highlights to the hair.

*Robert Kaufman Kona Cotton Sollids work well as flesh tones.*

*Robert Kaufman Multi-Dye fabrics work well as hair fabrics.*

LEFT **Quilting Diva** by Bonnie Lyn McCaffery. Full quilt on page 86.

### Tea Dyeing
1. Boil 4 cups of water. Steep two tea bags in the water for 2-3 minutes. Add a little cold water to cool it down.

2. Dip the pink fabric into the tea for just a few seconds. Check the color. Additional time in the cup of tea will intensify the tan coloring of the fabric.

3. Rinse in cool water.

4. Iron dry between two white colored, untextured paper towels.

The fabric is now ready to be painted.

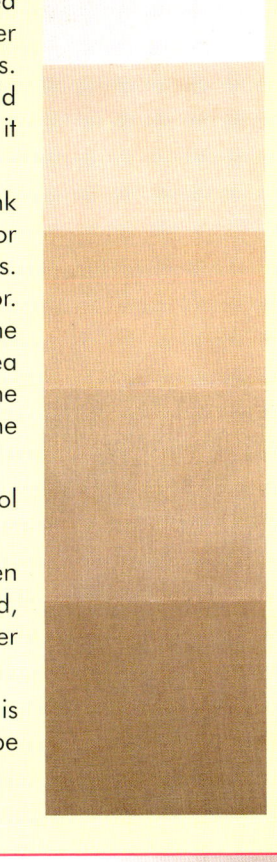

### Face Lining
The edges of the face and any flesh parts are turned under. To avoid the turned under seam allowance showing through, a lining is applied to the back of the painted face. I have experimented with a number of different fabrics, from plain white fabric to iron-on interfacings. Some of these products will wrinkle and cause facial wrinkling when quilted. I have found that lightweight iron-on interfacing or fusible fleece work nicely.

### Background
The background fabric is going to be the fabric that the face, hair, and clothing are set against. Select a color that will allow the hair and face to stand out. You can use any kind of fabric that you are comfortable stitching. Cottons are always a great choice, but various other fabrics will work as well. If it is stretchy knit type of fabric, it will need to be stabilized by fusing it to a lightweight interfacing.

### Sheer Overlay
The beauty of these painted face portraits is how easily the hair is made. Slivers and snips of fabric create hair-like texture. A layer of sheer tulle is necessary to hold the layers together without having to stitch every piece of fabric.

Tulle can cover the whole quilt top or it can just cover the hair area. The color of the tulle is important. Darker colored tulle is usually better than white or lighter colored tulle. The lighter colored tulle tends to make the colors beneath look washed out, while the darker colored tulle tends to intensify the colors underneath. If the flesh is going to be covered with the tulle, a brown or burgundy will keep the tone of the flesh in a warmer tone. If only the hair will be covered, select a color similar to the color of the hair.

It is worth experimenting with different colors of tulle. Do not lay the tulle directly on the evolving design. Instead, pull the design close to the edge of the table. Hold the tulle up with two hands, and capture the freely hanging tulle between your legs and the edge of the table. Extend your hands to hold the tulle at an angle over the design so that you can see through the tulle. You will be able to get an idea of how the color of the tulle is going to effect the color of the developing design.

### Borders
The border fabric can be any fabric you are comfortable stitching. Cottons are always a good choice. The color should compliment the background, as well as the face, hair, and clothing in the portrait. The decision for the border and binding fabric can be made after the central portrait has been completed. The portrait can be laid on top of different color choices to see which one sets the design off best.

### Backing and Batting
Cotton fabric is an excellent choice for the backing. A multicolored or busy print will camouflage the quilting stitches.

A low-loft batting works well with the painted face portraits. I like to use Pellon's Fusible Fleece. It has a very low loft and helps wall hangings hang flat. What I really appreciate is that it can be fused to the backing. This helps eliminate the worry of pleats in the backing while stitching the layers together.

# Paint Supplies

## Paints

I use DecoArt SoSoft Fabric Paints. These paints can be watered down with just water and applied to wet fabric to get a soft blend of color, or they can be used straight from the bottle on dry fabric to get a crisp fine line. They remain relatively soft to the hand and they do not need to be heat set. Pebeo Setacolor and PROfab Textile Paints also work but need to be heat set. Follow the manufacturer's directions.

Only a few colors are needed to get started on the face painting. The numbers listed refer to DecoArt SoSoft Fabric Paints.

- DSS41 Burnt Sienna – shading and eyebrows
- DSS38 Soft Red – base lip color
- DSS35 Soft Peach – highlights on the lip
- DSS1 White – whites of the eyes and the iris
- DSS24 Lamp Black – pupil, eyeliner and lashes
- DSS13 True Blue, DSS41 Burnt Sienna, or DSS44 True Green – iris
- DAS1 DecoArt Brush & Blend Extender is helpful in keeping the paint fluid and thin for painting very fine details. If you live in a dry climate, the extender is very helpful in keeping the paint wet longer.

You may add other colors later as you look at your photographs to see what colors are needed.

## Brushes

Good quality brushes are necessary to be able to get good results. Old brushes that have been used over the years may not give you some of the finer details on the face. It is worth purchasing new quality brushes to get the best results.

For a life-size painted face, I use just a couple of brushes. A size 4 or 5 round brush made of synthetic hairs can be used for most of the painting. It should come to a nice sharp clean point.

A fine liner brush (size 0 or 2/0) will produce very fine detail lines, eyelashes, and eyebrows. I like Loew-Cornell's American Painter 4000 Series.

A size 6 round brush is good for larger areas like the shading.

## Brush Care

Take good care of your brushes and they will last a long time. A few simple tips will keep your brushes in good shape.

If you are not using your brush, soak it in water to keep the paint from drying in the bristles. The brush can sit in water for a short time during a paint session, but should not be left in the water if you are done painting for the day.

Clean the brushes when you are done painting for the day. Use a brush cleaner for acrylic paints or put a dot of liquid hand soap in the palm of your hand. Roll the bristles of the brush in the soap and work the soap gently into the bristles by squeezing the bristles with your thumb and forefinger. Squeeze the bristles from the ferrule (the metal tube that holds the bristles on the brush) outward to the tips of the bristles. Do not scrub with the bristles. This will splay the hairs and they may never form a nice clean point again.

Work the soap into the bristles until the paint is removed.

Rinse in cool water.

Gently squeeze the excess water from the bristles.

Reshape the hairs of the brush into a point.

Allow the brush to dry either lying down or by hanging the brush with the hairs pointing downward. Do not allow any pressure on the hairs of the brush. This could cause them to be misshapen. Do not dry them by standing them with the bristles pointing upward. Any excess water will drain down into the ferrule. It will become trapped in the ferrule, causing the wooden handle to rot.

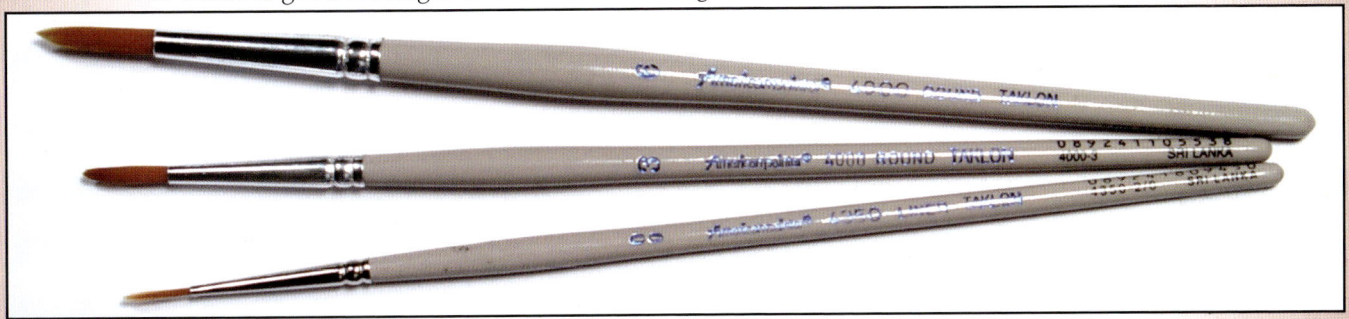

## Additional Painting Supplies

A few other supplies are needed for painting. You will need a stable cup for water. This should not be a drinking cup. Anything used for paints should not be used later for eating. Inexpensive clear plastic disposable cups work quite nicely for holding water. When you're done you can just throw it away. You will need a spray bottle to dampen the fabric during the wet-on-wet painting.

A disposable white plastic plate works very nicely as a palette. It should be white so you can clearly see the color of the paints without being influenced by the coloring of the plate. Plastic plates work better than Styrofoam. Styrofoam plates absorb the water too quickly.

White paper towels should be kept close-by for drying the paintbrush and rubbing off some of the paint while doing the dry brush painting. The paper towels will also be used to layer with the painted fabric while ironing the fabric dry. It is important to have paper towels without any print. This eliminates any worry of the ink on the paper towel ironing off onto the newly painted face. It is also best to have paper towels without any texture. The textured paper towels will sometimes leave the texture in the painted face fabric when it has been ironed dry between the paper towel layers.

You may also want a good light in your painting area. This will make it easier to see both the photograph from which you are working and the painting you are creating.

If you will be painting on a dark fabric that is difficult to see through, you may need a light box. A clear clipboard with a light below is a good substitute if you are painting a small area. I used a storm window balanced between two tables to paint "Abby's" jeans (on page 43), which were about 30" long.

A water soluble temporary marking pen is also helpful for transferring guidelines to the fabric after the wet-on-wet painting is ironed dry. Be sure to test on a scrap piece of fabric before using. Draw lines with the temporary marking pen. Stroke some paint over the lines. Let dry. Dab the temporary marks with water to be sure that they can be removed. If you decide to use the temporary marking pen on your fabric, be sure not to iron the fabric after it has been marked.

## Art Supplies

The secret to this technique is the guideline drawing. To paint the "Basic Beauty," I have provided the guideline drawing in the back of the book on page 89. Create a copy of this page. You can trace it on tracing paper with a permanent black pen, you can scan and print a copy of the page, or you can photocopy the page.

Once you are ready to paint the face of your choice, you will need a good photograph enlarged to the desired finished size of the face. The "Basic Beauty" photo is on page 88.

Use a clear plastic report cover to protect the guideline drawing from water during the painting process. The guideline drawing can also be traced directly on the clear report cover with a permanent black Sharpie pen.

## Sewing Supplies

A firm tear-away stabilizer is used under the background fabric. This serves to make the stitching look better. The stabilizer will need to be ironed flat. Be sure to select one that can be ironed, as there are some on the market that will disappear when ironed – and reappear on the iron surface.

Invisible thread is used to stitch the layered hair and clothing in place. It is also used to machine appliqué the finished edges of the face. There are many different brands of invisible thread available. Many are extremely difficult to use. I have taught many classes and have seen the wide variety of invisible threads that do not work well. The one that does work well is YLI Wonder Invisible Thread. It is important to stand this thread upright in the sewing machine. If you have a horizontal thread pin, you will need a thread stand in order for the machine to stitch properly. This thread does not like to lie down. You will also need to reduce the top tension on the sewing machine. A lower number is usually lower tension. Experiment with a piece of fabric and stabilizer to get the best tension setting.

The invisible thread is available in smoke and clear. If you are stitching something dark, use the smoke. Use clear for stitching light items. If you are unsure which to use, hold a single strand of thread over the item. If the thread is visible, you probably need to use the other color.

The bobbin thread should be similar in color to whatever is being stitched. I often use a neutral gray thread in the bobbin.

## Tools

A rotary cutter and cutting mat are very useful for cutting the fabrics. The mini rotary cutter is especially good for cutting curvy designs like hair. It cuts tight curves, but the disadvantage is that it can only cut through a few layers of fabric.

Fabric scissors are good to have available. These can be used in place of the rotary cutter and mat if you choose. The rotary cutter is preferable over the scissors for cutting clean-cut smooth curves. Cuts made with scissors may be jagged.

Spray starch is helpful to achieve clean-cut edges. The fabrics for the hair and clothing can be sprayed with starch on the back and ironed dry prior to being cut. This will help the fibers on the cut edge hold together.

A temporary fabric glue stick is needed to turn under the edges of the face.

A sewing machine with the ability to do free motion stitching is useful for stitching the layers together. If you are concerned that you do not have free motion experience on the sewing machine, this is an excellent opportunity for you to experiment with it since you will be stitching with invisible thread – so no one will know if you have not stitched it perfectly. If you do not have a free motion sewing machine foot, the stitching can be done with a standard sewing machine foot. It is more difficult because you will have to steer around every curve.

Be sure that your sewing machine is in good working order. They do need to be serviced and cleaned now and then. A yearly visit to the sewing machine service center will keep your machine running well and make for a much happier sewing experience.

A free motion or darning foot allows you to easily stitch the layers together with free motion stitching. These are available for specific sewing machine models and there are also generic versions available. You will need to know whether your sewing machine is a slant shank, low shank, or high shank before ordering the generic version.

A fine sewing machine needle is necessary with the invisible thread. The invisible thread is a very fine thread. If too large of a needle is used, a large hole is pierced into the fabric and the very fine invisible thread will not fill the hole. This makes the hole very visible. I recommend a size 70/10 needle for students.

Sewing machine needles should be changed after about 8 hours of use. If you are experiencing difficulty with the machine, the number one remedy is to try changing the needle.

# Preparation

## Photographs and Guideline Drawing Preparation

The secret to ease in painting the face is the guideline drawing positioned beneath the fabric. It is very easy to create a guideline drawing.

### Taking the Photo

Let me first make a comment about copyright. Professionally taken photos are copyrighted. If you plan on displaying your finished quilt in an exhibit, it is best to take your own photo to avoid any copyright infringement.

A good clear photo is necessary for painting the face. A photo can be selected from the many you have already taken. The difficulty with this is that the photos are often taken from a distance and details are not clearly visible. You will have more control over the quality if you take a photo especially for the purpose of painting a face.

### Photo Preparation

Enlarge the face photo to the desired finished size of the face you want to paint. I recommend that the finished size of the face be slightly smaller than life-size. I prefer not to add heavy quilting to the face. A large finished face will leave too much area unquilted and may look monstrous.

If you have a digital camera or scanner and color printer, you may be able to print your own enlarged photo. Otherwise, an office supply store will be able to make a color enlargement. It is important that the photo be enlarged in color as this will be a reference tool while painting. It will be much easier to copy if your brain does not have to do a re-sizing calculation.

The color photo can also be scanned into a computer, enlarged, and printed out in color if you have the tools available. You may also want to make a black and white copy of the enlarged photo. This is a helpful tool for seeing the shading.

If you are experienced with a computer "paint" type program, you can convert the color photo to gray scale and posterize the photo or apply a "Gaussian Blur" and increase the contrast in the gray scale photo. Reduce the number of colors to eight to ten colors. Experiment to see what works best. This will create a very good graphic example of the areas in shades of gray.

I have included the color and black and white photographs on pages 88 and 18 for the "Basic Beauty".

### Tips for good photos

- Take photos outdoors on an overcast, but bright day. This will offer the best lighting to get natural color and soft shadows. Position the subject in a shaded area to avoid high contrast shadows. Deep shadows will hide features of the face, making it very difficult to paint.
- The subject should stand in front of a background that will contrast with their hair and face. This will make it much easier to see the shape of the face and hair.
- Take a close-up photo of the subjects face. If you use a close-up feature on the camera, this will avoid having to stand so close to the subject that they feel uncomfortable.
- Take several photos from different angles and with various facial expressions. This will give you a variety of photos to choose from.
- A closed mouth is much easier to paint for the first time.
- Take additional photos of the subject posing in order to get reference photos for the rest of the body.

## Preparing the Guideline Drawing

A guideline drawing is provided for the "Basic Beauty on page 89.

**1** Slide the enlarged color photo into a clear plastic report cover. Use a black permanent pen to outline the shape of the face and head. Draw additional lines for the facial features - the outline of the lips, the outline of the nose, and the outline of the features in the eye. Draw lines where there are any strong contrasts in color. Lines are also drawn where there are strong shadows or bright areas of highlight. I like to use dotted lines where there are subtle shadings or highlights. The guideline drawing lines will be necessary for determining the placement of the facial features, shadows, and highlights. Draw lines wherever necessary to show you areas of change. This will not be a pretty drawing.

**2** Add two large "+" signs to opposite corners of the report covers to act as registration marks. Position these in areas outside of the face. These will be used to realign the fabric later.

**3** Remove the photo from the report cover. Replace it with a plain white piece of paper. The white piece of paper is needed to see the lines you have just drawn.

### Setup to Paint
You are ready to paint the face. Gather your supplies. You will need:

- DecoArt SoSoft Fabrics Paints
    DSS41 Burnt Sienna – shading and eyebrows
    DSS38 Soft Red – base lip color
    DSS35 Soft Peach – highlights on the lip
    DSS1 White – whites of the eyes and the iris
    DSS24 Lamp Black
    – pupil, eyeliner and lashes
    DSS13 True Blue,
    DSS41 Burnt Sienna,
    or DSS44 True Green
    – iris
    DAS1 Brush & Blend Extender
- Brushes
    Size 6 round brush
    Size 4 or 5 round brush
    Size 0 fine liner brush
- Plastic plate palette
- Cup of clean water
- A paper towel
- Color reference photo
- Black and white copy of the reference photo
- Spray bottle of water
- Masking tape
- Pencil
- Flesh colored fabric, washed and ironed to remove any finish on the fabric. Cut large enough to cover the area to be painted.
- Guideline drawing – for the "Basic Beauty" you will need to make a copy or trace the guideline drawing on a report cover with a permanent black pen as described on page 14.
- Clear report cover or page protector.

**1** The guideline drawing provided for the "Basic Beauty" is on page 89. Make a copy and slide this into a clear report cover to protect it from the water. If you create your own guideline drawing on paper, slide it into a report cover to protect it from the water. If you draw your own guideline drawing on the report cover, place a piece of plain white paper in the report cover to make the guideline drawing more visible.

**2** Use two pieces of masking tape to tape the guideline drawing to the back of the flesh colored fabric. Be sure that the fabric lays flat against the guideline drawing.

**3** Position the prepared fabric in front of you. If you are right-handed, place the palette and cup of water to the right of the fabric. Those who are left-handed should place the palette and cup of water to the left of the fabric. Fold a paper towel in half and set next to or below the palette. Place the reference photos on the opposite side of the cup and palette. I like to have the bottles of paint handy above the palette and cup.

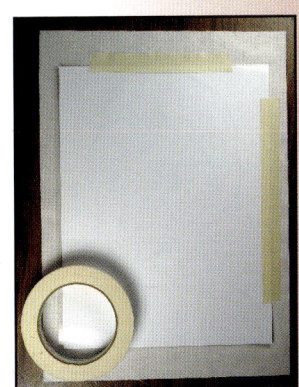

## Wet-on-Wet Painting Technique

Painting watered-down paint on wet fabric creates soft shading on the fabric. This is useful for painting the shading on the face.

**1** Spray the fabric with water until the fabric is very damp, but not dripping wet. It should feel moist to the touch. Wetting the fabric will allow the paint to bleed and flow. This will give a soft blending effect for shading.

**2** Using the size 6 round brush, pick up some water and bring it to the palette. Begin by swirling the brush in a circular motion about ½" from the dot of paint. Pull the brush along the very edge of the dot of paint, picking up a tiny bit of color. Pick up more water from the cup of water. Do not wipe the brush on the edge of the cup. Bring it back to the palette to swirl into the watered down paint. This will thin the paint down. You want to work with very watered down color to start. A better way to describe it would be water with a tiny bit of color added. You will be able to add more pigment later.

**3** Test the watered down paint mixture on the paper towel. It should be a very light watered down version of the brown paint. If it is too dark, continue to add water to the paint mixture. If it is too light, pick up more water with the brush and pull a tiny bit of paint into the watered down paint mixture. It is better to have the color too light than too dark. If the color looks good, do a test stroke of color on the fabric in an area that will not be used (either the background or the scalp area). The color should flow on the damp fabric. Adjust the water/paint mixture as necessary. The color of the watered down paint will lighten when it is dry.

**4** Wiggle, press, and pull the brush as it comes in contact with the fabric. This will blend the paint into the fabric. Paint only a few strokes at a time before reloading the brush. Dip first into the water and then into the water/paint mixture. If it needs to be darker, pull the brush through the edge of the paint as described above. Start by painting with a light watered down mixture of paint. You will be able to darken areas later by adding a little more paint to the mixture.

# SECTION II: Let's Paint
## Shading the Face

### Painting the Face

This section covers the techniques you need to paint a face. I encourage you to paint the "Basic Beauty" following the steps below. Additional facial features (freckles, wrinkles, moles, and teeth) are also included in this section for when you start painting your own face of choice.

### Shading

You are now ready to start painting. You can do this! Please note that all references to left and right refer to the photograph, not the photographed person's left or right.

1. Spray the fabric with water until the fabric is very damp, but not dripping wet. Mark the two registration marks on the flesh colored fabric with a pencil. These will be used to reposition the fabric once the shading is done.

2. Use the color photograph and the black and white copy as a reference. Carefully look at each area of the photograph before you paint. Look to see where the shading is and how dark it is. Learn to look for the darkest and lightest areas of the flesh. The black and white copy of the photograph is very helpful. This makes it much easier to see the darkest and the lightest areas.

3. Use the black and white photo only as a guide and be sure that the painted colors blend. A gray scale photo has been included for the "Basic Beauty" on page 18. The lightest areas will be kept free of paint. Darker areas will need more paint added.

4. Squeeze a drop of Burnt Sienna on the palette. A small dot of paint is all that is needed. Create a puddle of very watered-down paint as described in the section on Wet-on-Wet Painting on page 16. Always test in an inconspicuous area to be sure that the paint mixture is not too dark.

**Shading**

**Paint Colors:**
- DSS41 Burnt Sienna

**Brushes:**
- size 6 round brush

**oops!**

**How to Fix It**

If you paint an area by mistake that you wish to leave lighter, immediately dip the brush into water and touch the brush to the mistake. This will water down the paint in the fabric. Blot with paper towel to lift out some of the color. This must be done immediately to get the color out. It will not work if there is too much pigment in the watered down paint mixture.

Note: The numbered areas are referenced in the step-by-step shading instructions.

5 A good area to start adding shading is at the hairline. Look at the photo to see where there is shading and then look back at the fabric (with the guideline below) to locate this area. Notice the shading where the hair meets the forehead. (1)

6 Look at the eye area next. Notice that there is shading both above (2) and below the eye (3). It is important to paint what you see and not what you know. You may think that painting shadows under the eyes will make her appear to be tired and old, but it is the shading that adds the dimension to the face. Notice the light shading above and between the eyebrows (4). Paint the shading around the eyes. There are shadows near the nose (5). Do not worry if paint flows into the eye area. This will be painted over later.

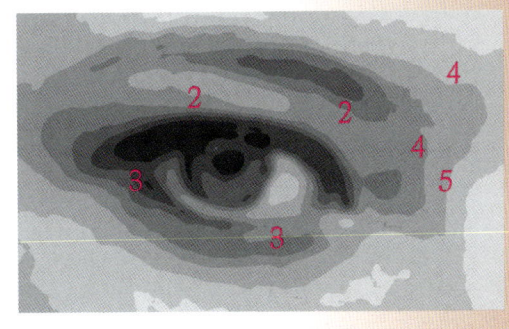

7 Look now at the nose. There are light shadows to the right and left of the nose (6). These help to delineate the nose from the face. Take care to leave the highlighted part of the nose unpainted (7). Notice the shading around the nostrils (8). The area under the tip of her nose is also darker (9). Paint this shading. Do not worry about making the nostril holes dark. Additional shading will be done on the nose later. Take note of the shadow below her nose (10). It is in a triangular shape.

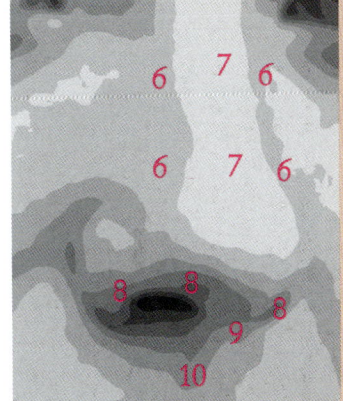

8 Notice also the shading on the right cheek (11). This side of the face is lighter than the left side. Add shading as you see it. Allow the paint to flow beyond the edge of her face into the background area. There is shading on the far left cheek (12). Notice how the left cheek area has a "smile" shaped cup of shading below the highlight area (12). Add light shading below the highlight area to make the highlight stand out.

9 Add a little shading to the ear (13). It does not have to be very detailed, just darker than the other areas.

10 Look now at the area around the mouth. You do not need to shade the mouth itself at this time – just the skin area around the mouth. Do not worry if the shading flows into the mouth area. This will be painted over later. There is some shading along the smile lines on the cheek (14). Notice how these smile creases travel right up to the corner of the nostril (14). Notice how the area above the upper lip has a little light shading (15). The area just below her lower lip has some darker shading (16).

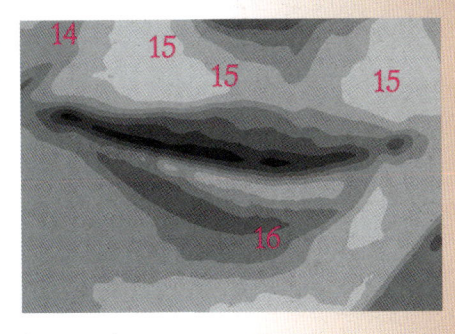

11 Now look at her chin and jaw line. Notice the light shading midway between her mouth and chin (17) while there is a small highlighted area below the right lower lip (18). Right of her chin (19) and the ball of her chin (20) have some shading. Shading along the jaw line on the left will help delineate her face from her neck (21).

12 The neck and face have some shading above and below her chin (22). Add the shading as you see it. Notice that there is some shading to the left of the neck on the shoulder area (23). This helps to delineate the neck from the shoulder.

13 Once you have painted the shading, go back and add darker shading wherever you see the need. Carefully look at each area again. Keep in mind that it will dry lighter.

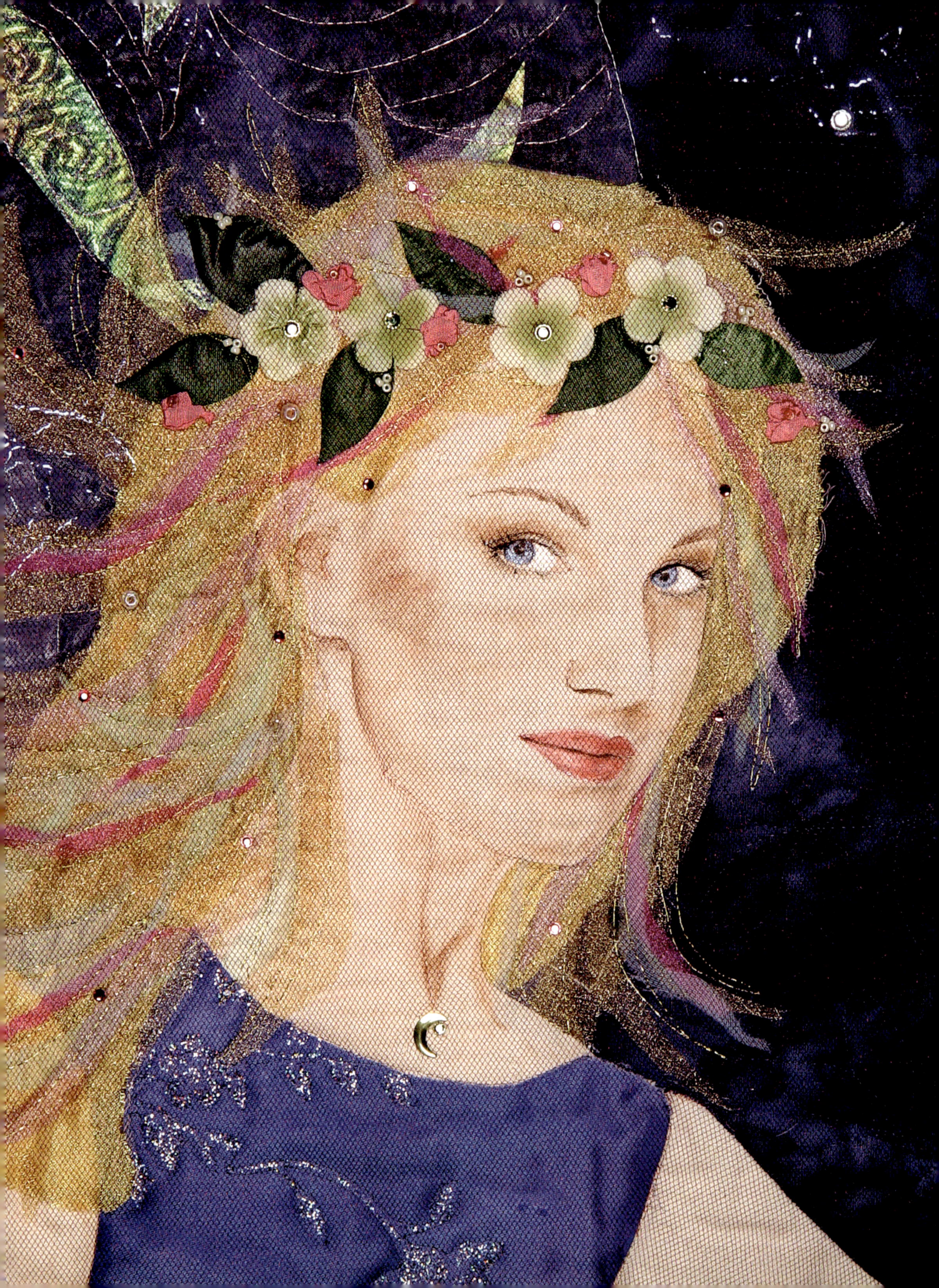

# Iron Dry

**1** The shading is the only part of the face that is done with this wet-on-wet technique. It is necessary to iron the fabric dry. Temporarily remove the guideline drawing from the back of the fabric. Be sure you have added the registration marks before removing the fabric from the guideline drawing. Lay the fabric on a clean paper towel and cover with another clean paper towel. Iron until the fabric is completely dry. Any dampness that remains in the fabric will make the paint bleed and this is not desired for the remaining painting. Be sure it is bone dry.

If you decide that the shading is too light, the wet-on-wet painting process can be repeated. Spray the fabric with water and add more watered down shading. Iron the fabric dry.

**2** Wipe the guideline drawing with a paper towel to remove any paint residue. If you forget to do this, the droplets of paint left from the painting will be picked up by the newly ironed dry fabric.

**3** Reposition the fabric back onto the guideline drawing. Use the registration marks to carefully position it. Tape the guideline drawing to the back of the fabric. You are now ready to paint the features of the face.

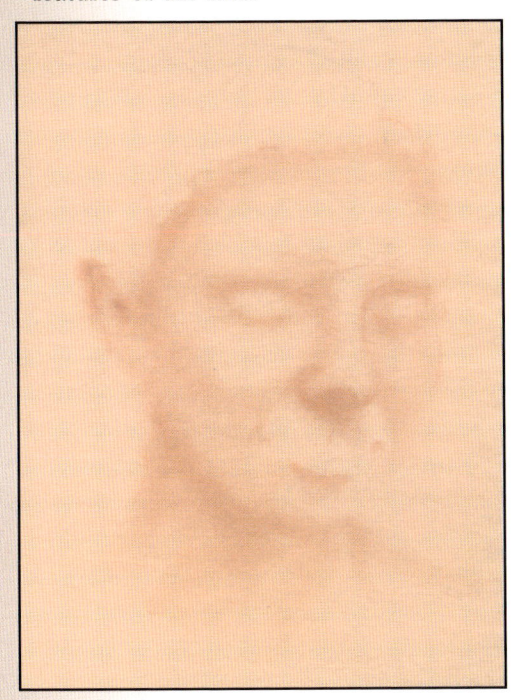

*LEFT close-up* **Contemplation III: Oh Just To Be** *by Bonnie Lyn McCaffery. Full quilt shown on page 4.*

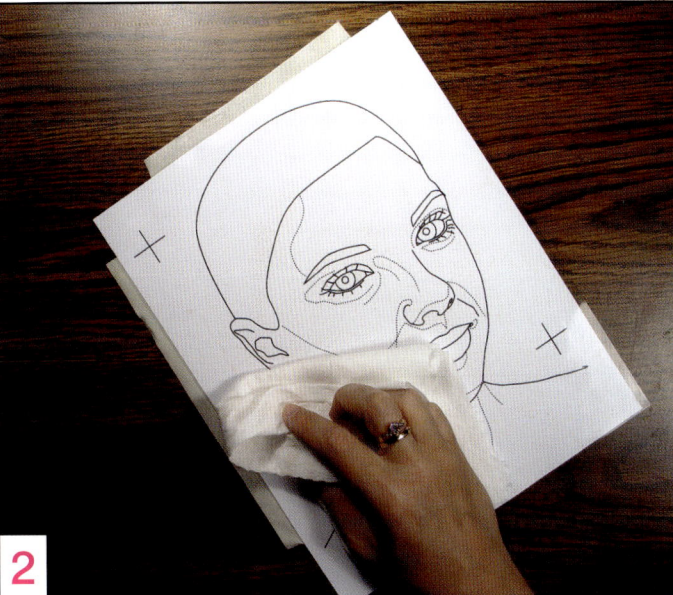

21

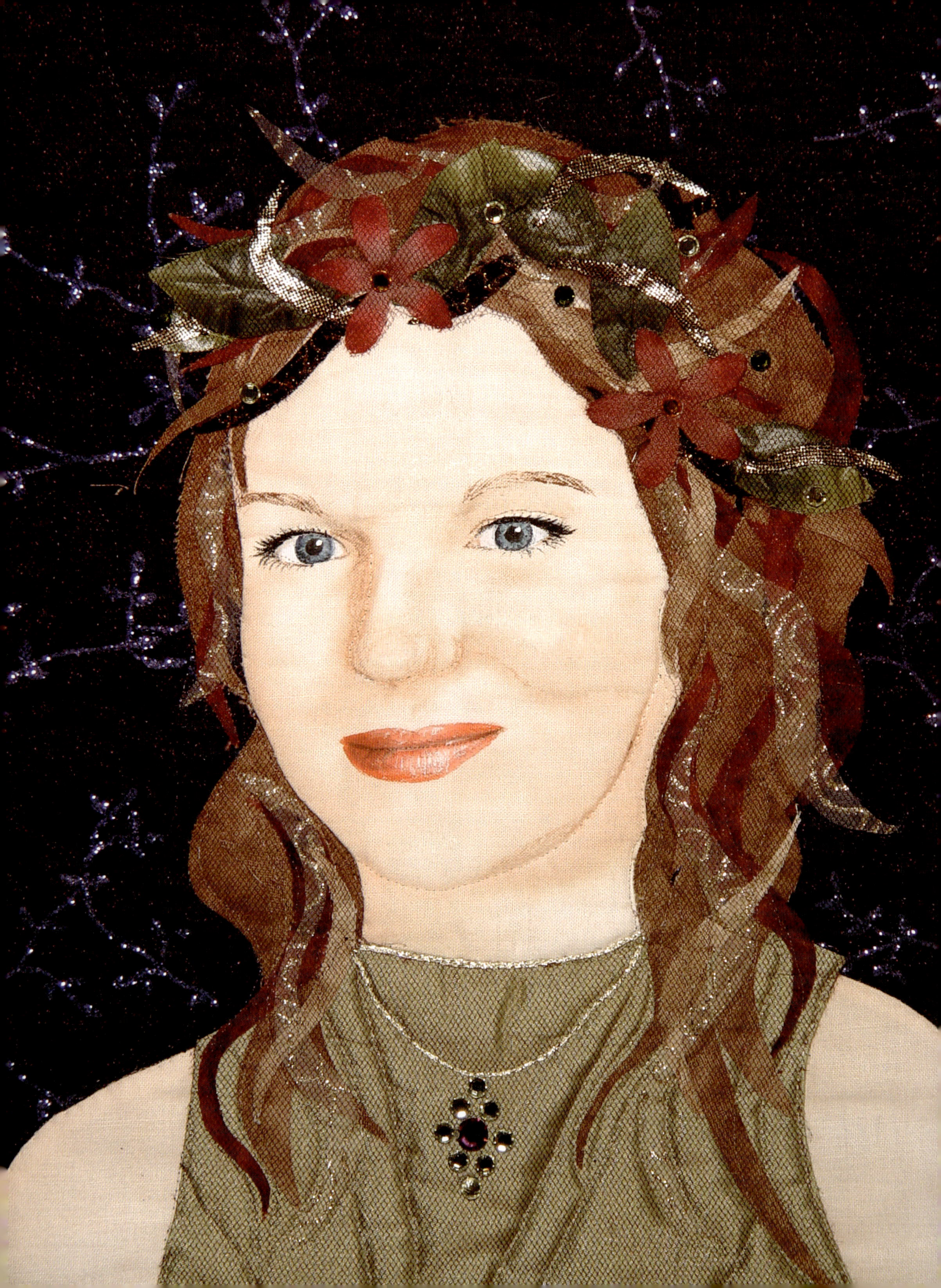

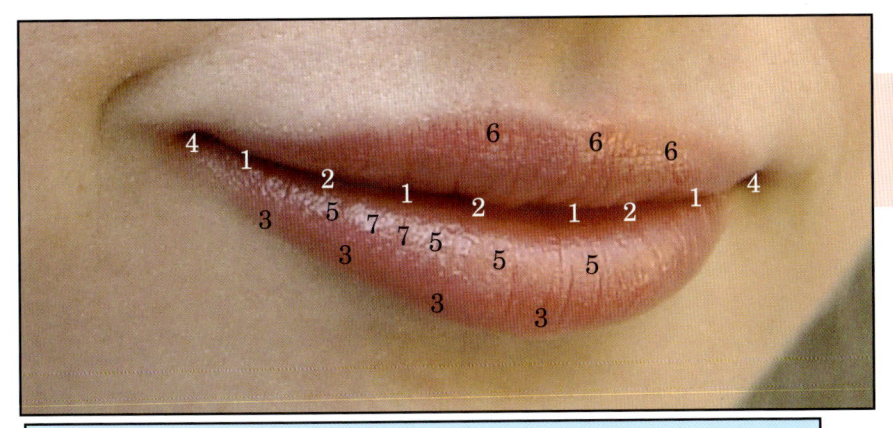

# Lips

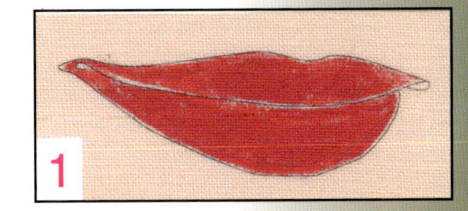

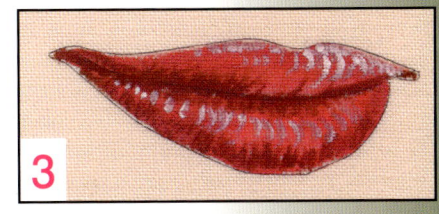

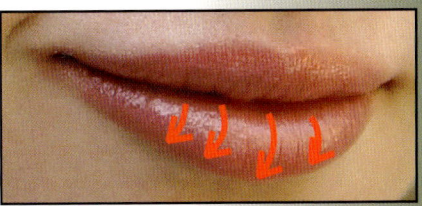

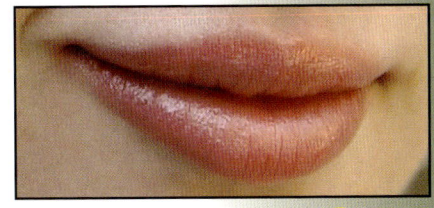

**IMPORTANT NOTE:** From this point forward, the paint will be used without adding any water to it. Do not water down the paint because this will cause it to bleed into the dry fabric. If the paint dries too quickly, dip the brush in the extender before dipping into the paint. This will keep the paint from drying too quickly.

### Lips

**Paint Colors:**
- DSS38 Soft Red
- DSS35 Soft Peach
- DSS41 Burnt Sienna
- DAS1 Brush & Blend Extender

**Brushes:**
- size 4 or 5 round brush

The lips are done with a paint on paint blending technique.

**1** Paint a base coat of Soft Red within the lines of the lips. It is important to stay within the lines, as it is not possible to make corrections outside the lines. If you paint outside the lines, you will have to make the lips bigger to compensate for the error. Try to leave a very thin line between the lips free of paint (1).

**2** Immediately add the shading to the lips. Do not let the Soft Red paint dry before adding the shading. If it drys too quickly, repaint the base coat with a mixture of Soft Red and Extender. Without cleaning the brush, pick up a tiny amount of Burnt Sienna. Add Burnt Sienna to the thin line between the two lips. Add some shading where the upper and lower lips come together (2). Brush a few strokes of Burnt Sienna on the bottom of the lower lip. Follow the curve of the lip (3). Blend the Burnt Sienna into the Soft Red by stroking over it. Notice the dark corners of the mouth (4). Add Burnt Sienna to these places and blend well.

**3** Without cleaning the brush, pick up a little Soft Peach on the tip of the brush. This will be used to add highlights to the lips. Notice the highlights on the full part of the lower lip (5). It runs along the fullness of her lower lip. Brush a few strokes and blend it into the Soft Red. Use curved comma strokes to help keep the contour of the lower lip. Use a little Soft Peach to soften the top right and center of the upper lip (6).

**4** Blend the colors. Use a little less blending to keep the strong highlighted area on the lower lip (7).

NOTE: The color of the lips can be changed by mixing paint colors. Lighten by mixing Soft Peach with the Soft Red before painting the base coat. Men's lips might be better colored by using a mixture of Soft Red, Burnt Sienna, and Soft Peach.

*LEFT close-up* **Contemplation IV** *by Bonnie Lyn McCaffery. Full quilt on page 54.*

### oops!

**How to Fix It**

It is important to stay within the lines while painting the lips, as it is not possible to make corrections to areas painted outside the lines. If you paint outside the lines, you will have to make the lips bigger to compensate for the error.

Errors within the lines of the lips can just be painted over.

23

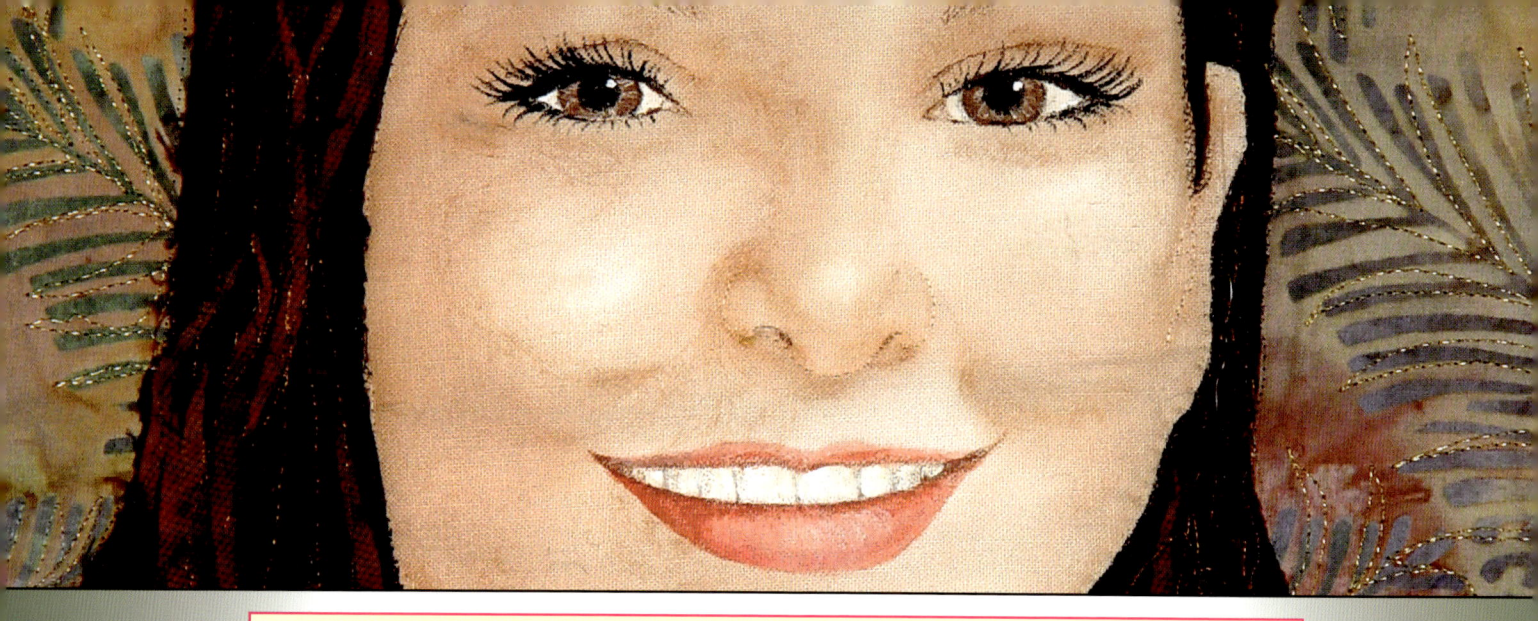

### Dry Brush Technique

This technique is useful for adding shading that is a little stronger in color than the wet-on-wet shading. You may want to practice on an unused area of the fabric until you are comfortable with it.

Dry brushing is done with a "dirty" brush. Loading the brush is similar to the way it is done for stenciling. It is called off-loading the paint. Make sure the brush is very dry. Any moisture in the brush will make the paint look darker as you paint.

1 First load the brush with a little Burnt Sienna by brushing the paintbrush back and forth. Take care not to get paint in the ferrule.

2 Work some of the paint off the brush by rolling and wiggling the bristles on a paper towel. Roll the brush so the paint is removed from all sides of the brush. Stroke the brush several times on the paper towel until most of the paint is removed. The brush is properly loaded when there is just the barest trace of soft color being left behind. A student described this as a "dirty" brush. Too little paint is better than too much. Test on an area that will not be used (either the background or the scalp area.)

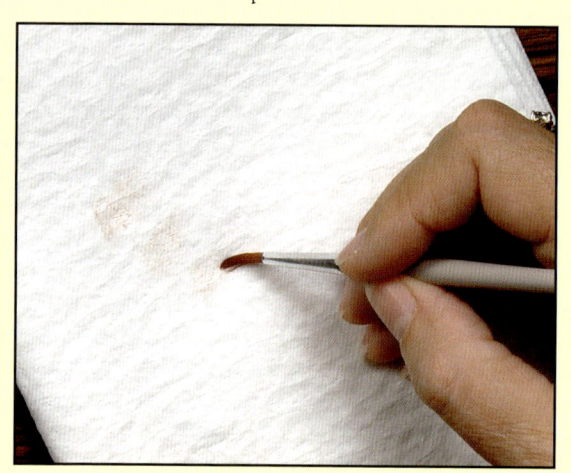

Use short, wiggling strokes and a very light hand to add additional shading to the nose and eye area.

**oops!**

### How to Fix It

It is very difficult to correct errors done with the dry brush technique. Use a very light hand and always test on the paper towel each time after loading the brush with paint. It is better to paint too light rather than too dark. You can always make it darker.

# Nose & Eye Shading

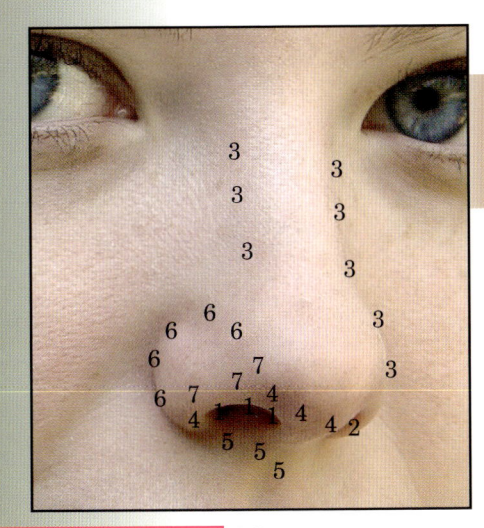

**Nose & Eye Shading**

**Paint Colors:**
- DSS41 Burnt Sienna

**Brushes:**
- size 4 or 5 round brush

## Nose

**1** Paint the nostril area with a little Burnt Sienna. Notice how there is a hard edge along the top edge of the left nostril and the color grows lighter as it goes down (1). Use lighter pressure on the brush to reduce the amount of paint that is left behind on the fabric. The right nostril is just a fine line (2).

**2** Use a very light handed dry brushing technique (described on page 24) to add some soft shading along the right and left side of the nose (3). Notice the shadows under the tip of the nose (4), under the left nostril (5), and along the left edge of the nostril (6). There is also some light shading that creates the roundness of the left nostril (7). Refer back and forth with the color reference photo.

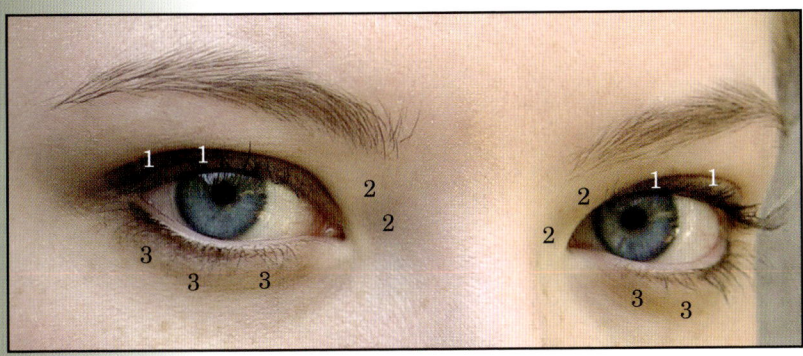

## Additional Shading in the Eye Area

**1** While your brush is loaded for dry brush shading, add more shading to the eye area. The shading of the eye area is done using the same dry brush painting technique used for the nose. Add any additional shading that is needed. It is often necessary to add some shading along the crease in the upper eye (1), on the inside curve near the nose (2), and just below the eye (3).

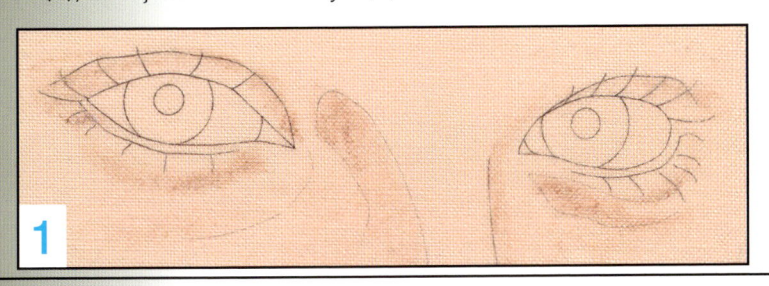

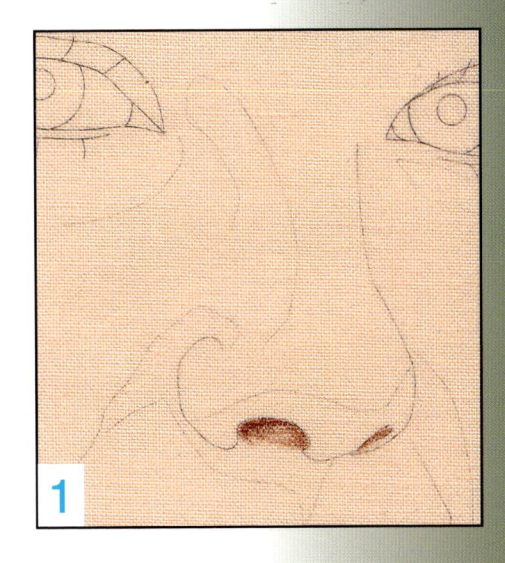

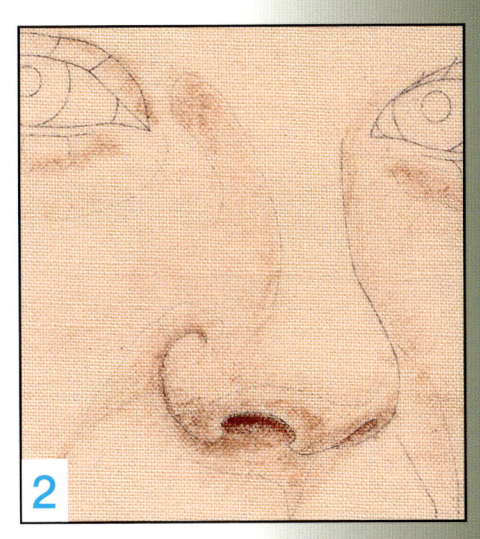

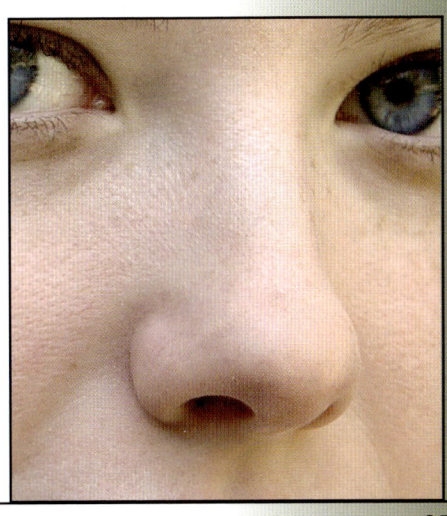

25

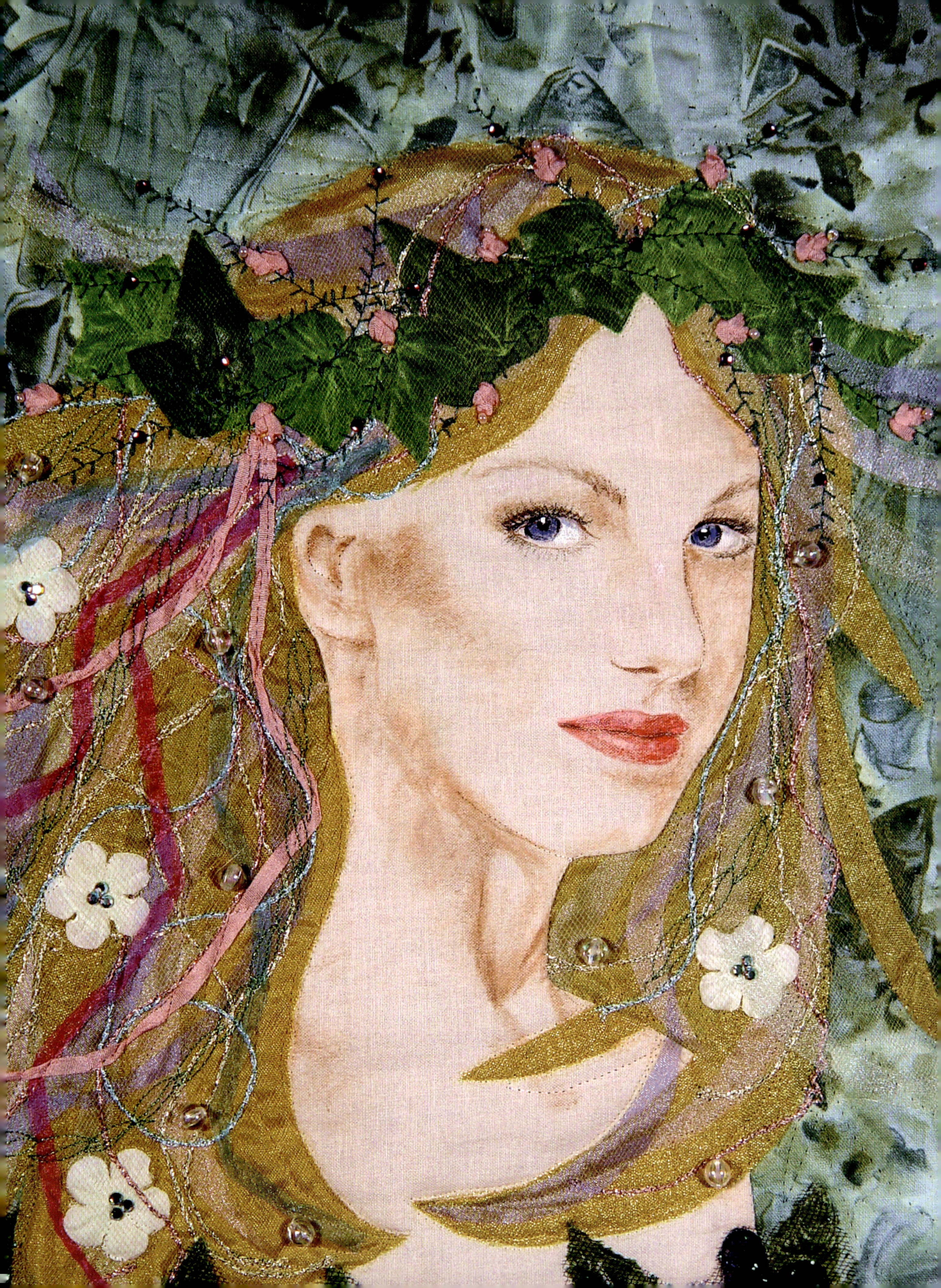

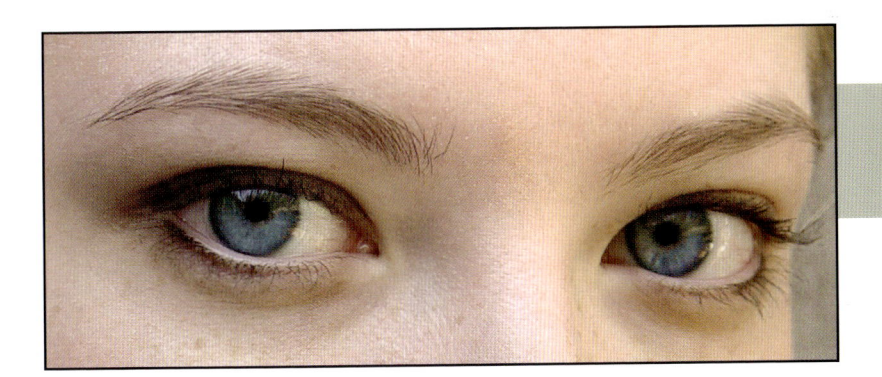

# Eyes

TIP If you have difficulty seeing the guidelines, press the fabric down so it is in contact with the guideline drawing. If this trick does not work, draw the lines with a disappearing blue pen using a light box. Once the paint is dry, dab the lines with clear water to remove them.

**Iris**
**Paint Colors:**
- DSS1 White
- DSS24 Black
- Eye color (DSS13 True Blue used in the example)
- DAS1 Brush & Blend Extender

**Brushes:**
- size 4 or 5 round brush

## Painting the Iris

**1** Paint one iris at a time. Paint the pupil Black. Notice that the iris is a circle, but the eyelid cuts it off. (1A) Paint a ring of Black around the outside of the iris. The black outer ring will stop where the eyelid cuts off the top edge of the iris (1B).

**2** Without cleaning the brush, paint a ring of True Blue (or whatever color you choose for the eye color) within the outer Black ring.

**3** Without cleaning the brush, paint a White ring between the True Blue ring and the pupil.

**4** Wipe the brush on a paper towel to remove most of the paint. You do not need to wash it out with water. Pull the tip of the brush from the outer ring in through the pupil. Think of these lines as the spokes on a wheel. Pull lines in different areas of the circle. Think of the circle as a clock. Start dragging a line at 12 o'clock. Then paint at 3, 6, and 9. Next move to 1 o'clock and rotate moving every 3 hours. This helps achieve flecks of color in the iris. It is okay to pull the lines right into the pupil – which will distort the painting done in the pupil. This will be repainted shortly. If it dries too quickly, repaint each color with a little Extender mixed into the paint. Repeat the pulling of the colors described above.

Continue to pull lines around the whole circle. Try not to blend the colors too much. It is much more realistic looking to have the flecks of color in the iris. If the eye color becomes too muddied, more eye color can be picked up on the brush and pulled from the outer ring into the pupil. Paint one iris completely. Then paint the iris of the other eye.

**5** After both irises are painted, repaint the pupils black. It is important that pupils and irises be painted the same size on each eye. The pupil is a circle centered in the middle of the iris.

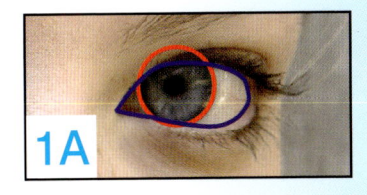

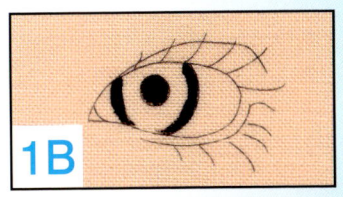

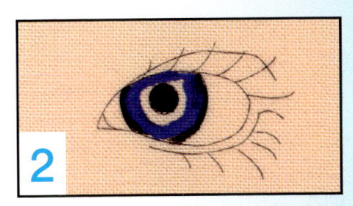

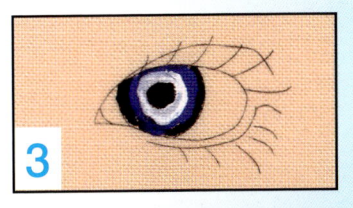

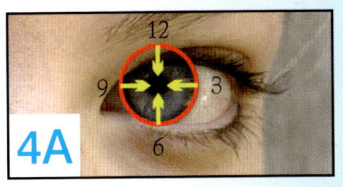

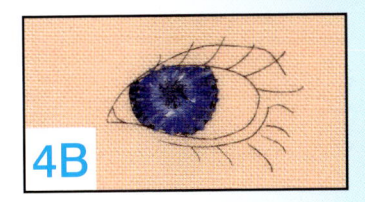

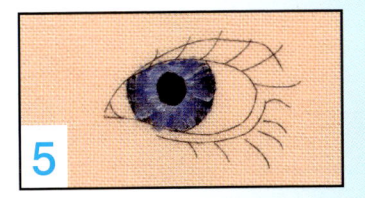

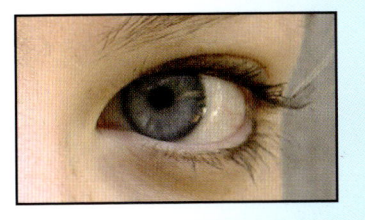

*LEFT close-up* **Adam's Yve St. Laurent** *by Bonnie Lyn McCaffery. Full quilt on page 69.*

27

**Whites of the Eye**

**Paint Colors:**
- DSS1 White
- DSS41 Burnt Sienna
- DAS1 Brush & Blend Extender

**Brushes:**
- size 4 or 5 round brush
- size 0 - fine liner brush

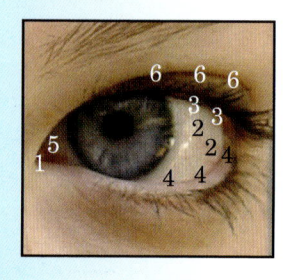

## Painting the Whites of the Eyes

**1** Paint the white of the eye with White paint. Look carefully at the photograph. Repaint with a mixture of White and Extender if it dries too quickly. Do not paint the tear duct area with the White (1).

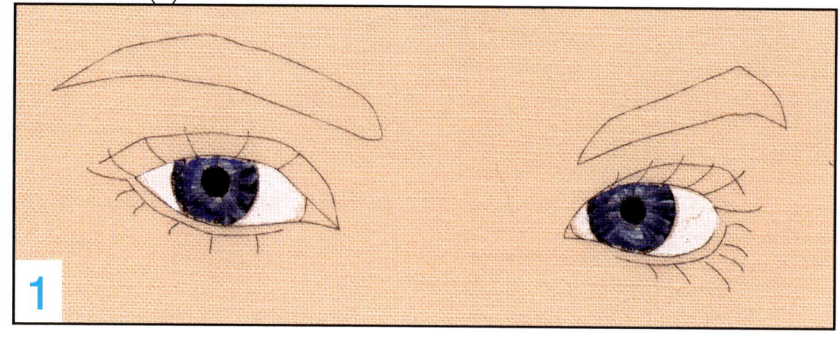

**2** Without cleaning the brush, pick up a tiny touch of Burnt Sienna. Blend this into the white of the eye to add shading. There is some shading along the outer edge of the eye (2) and below the upper eyelashes (3). Add more white if it becomes too dark. Wipe most of the paint from the brush. Pick up some Burnt Sienna with the fine liner brush and roll the brush point to a sharp point. Paint a fine line along the inside rim of the lower eyelid (4). Add a little Burnt Sienna to the tear duct area (5). This area should not be a solid area of paint. It should be a combination of lining the area with paint and dry brushing the area. Pick up more Burnt Sienna. Roll the brush point to a sharp point. Paint the crease on the upper eyelid (6). Wash out the brush.

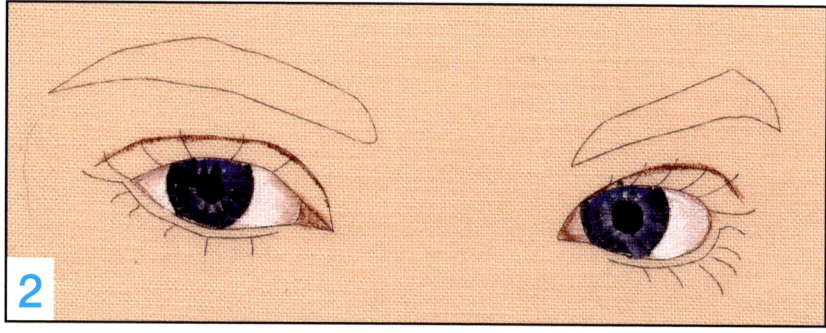

### How to Fix It

Areas painted with solid colored paint can be corrected by just painting over them. Eyelashes and eyebrows cannot be corrected. Take care to test out the fine liner stroke before painting the lashes or brows.

**oops!**

28

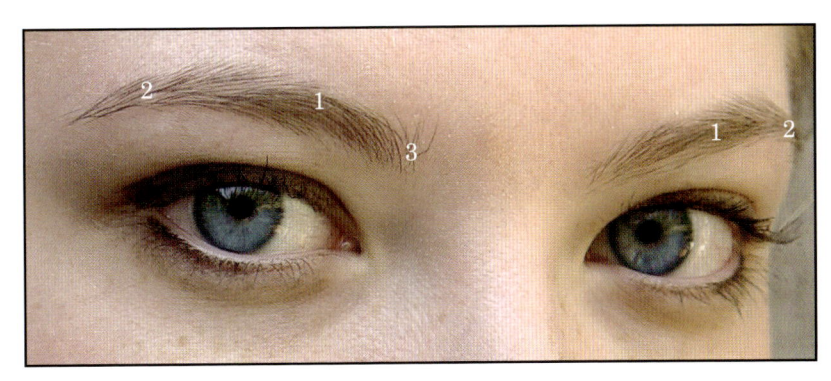

## Eyebrows

**Paint Colors:**
- DAS1 Brush & Blend Extender
- DSS41 Burnt Sienna

**Brushes:**
- size 0 - fine liner brush

## Eyebrows

**1** Load the brush with Burnt Sienna as described in the "Painting Fine Lines" instructions below. Eyebrow hairs are usually straighter than eyelashes. The eyebrows are usually denser near the center of the face (1) and fewer as they move to the outer edge of the face (2). Take care to paint the eyebrow hair in the direction it grows. Look carefully at the photograph. Notice how the hairs start in one direction and gradually slant more as they move to the outer edge of the face. Also notice that a few hairs grow in an awkward direction at the center of the face (3). Paint a few very light hairs growing up and towards the nose. This will give the painting a very realistic detail.

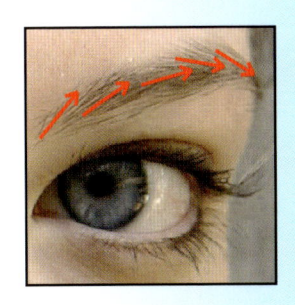

Clean the brush thoroughly.

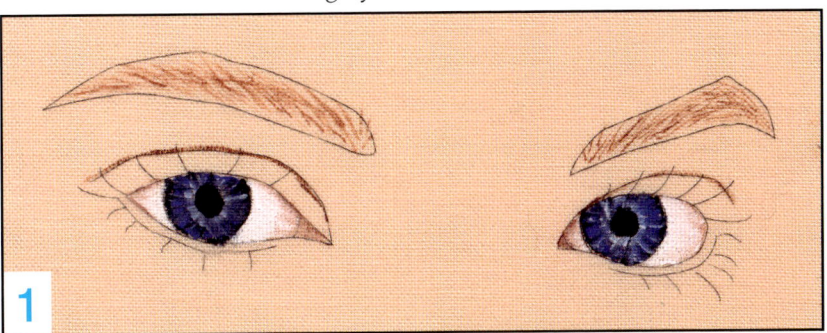

## Painting Fine Lines

A very fine liner brush is used to paint fine lines such as eyebrows and eyelashes. Use a small amount of Brush & Blend Extender with the paint to keep the paint flowing. Do not add water, as this will cause the paint to bleed into the fabric. ALWAYS use a fresh drop of paint when painting fine lines. The paint begins to dry out as soon as it is on the palette and it is important that it flow in order to paint fine, clean lines.

Pick up a drop of Brush & Blend Extender with the brush and mix it into a little of the paint color. Orient the brush at a 10 to 15 degree angle from the palette surface. Roll a fine point on the brush by rolling and pulling the brush. Lift the pressure as you pull away until the tip of the brush is off the palette.

Hold the paintbrush angled low to the surface. Position the brush tip at the widest end of the stroke (such as the base of an eyelash). Pull and lift the brush to the end of the stroke (such as the tip of the eyelash). The brush will not hold very much paint, so it is important to reload the brush often. You will probably be able to paint two to three eyelash or eyebrow hairs per brush load.

Extender is very helpful in keeping the paint flowing. Pick up a tiny bit of Brush & Blend Extender each time the paintbrush is reloaded with paint.

**Eyelashes & Eyeliner**

**Paint Colors:**
- DAS1 Brush & Blend Extender
- DSS24 Black

**Brushes:**
- size 0 - fine liner brush

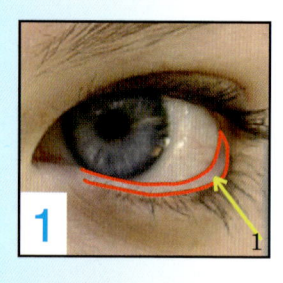

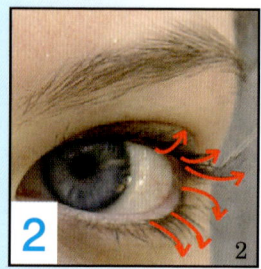

## Eyelashes & Eyeliner

**1** Load the brush with Black as described in the "Painting Fine Lines" instructions on page 29. Start by painting the eyeliner above the eye. Notice how the line is very fine near the nose and becomes wider near the outer edge of the eye. It is important to look carefully at the lower eyeliner and position of the lower lashes. There is a thin rim of flesh between the eyeball and the lower lashes (1). Paint the lower eyeliner with a very light hand. Notice that the eyeliner begins at the outer edge of the eye and does not extend all the way to the nose area. It only extends about halfway.

**2** The eyelashes are painted using the same stroke as the eyebrows. Load the fine liner brush to paint the eyelashes. Start the paint stroke along the eyeliner and lift and pull as you pull outward and up. Look very carefully at the curve of the eyelash. Eyelashes usually have a nice gentle curve – they are not straight lines (2). Also notice that the eyelashes become shorter as they get closer to the nose. Paint a few eyelashes spread across the top eyelid. Reload the brush and fill in the lash area. Eyelashes are not all the same length. Be sure to vary the lengths to give a realistic look.

**3** Look carefully at the lower eyelashes. They are much shorter and sparser. They only extend about halfway along the outer edge of the lower eyelid. Do not forget to leave the flesh colored rim of the eye free of lashes. Paint a few lashes below the eye with a very light hand. Lower lashes are much finer.

## Highlights

**Highlights**

**Paint Colors:**
- White

**Brushes:**
- size 0 - fine liner brush

**4** It is amazing what this tiny dot of white on the eyeball will do. This will make the eyes come to life. Decide where to position the highlight. It should be located somewhere on the iris or pupil. Think of the iris as the face of a clock. Select "a time" to position the dot on one eye – let's say 1:00. Pick up a tiny dot of White paint on the tip of the fine liner brush. Touch the tip of the brush at 1:00 where the pupil meets the iris to leave a dot of paint at the selected "time" position. Paint a dot on the other eye in the same location.

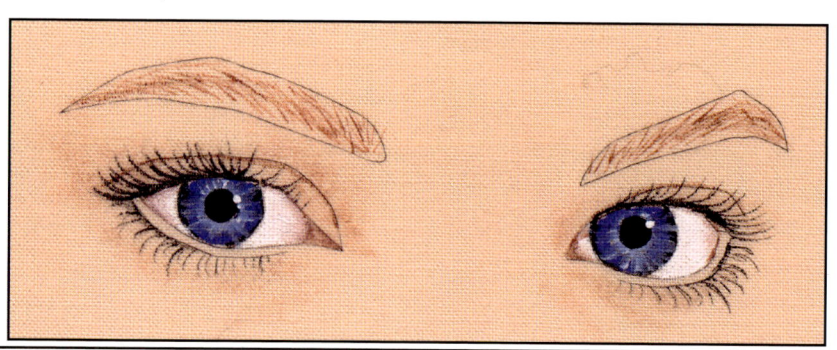

30

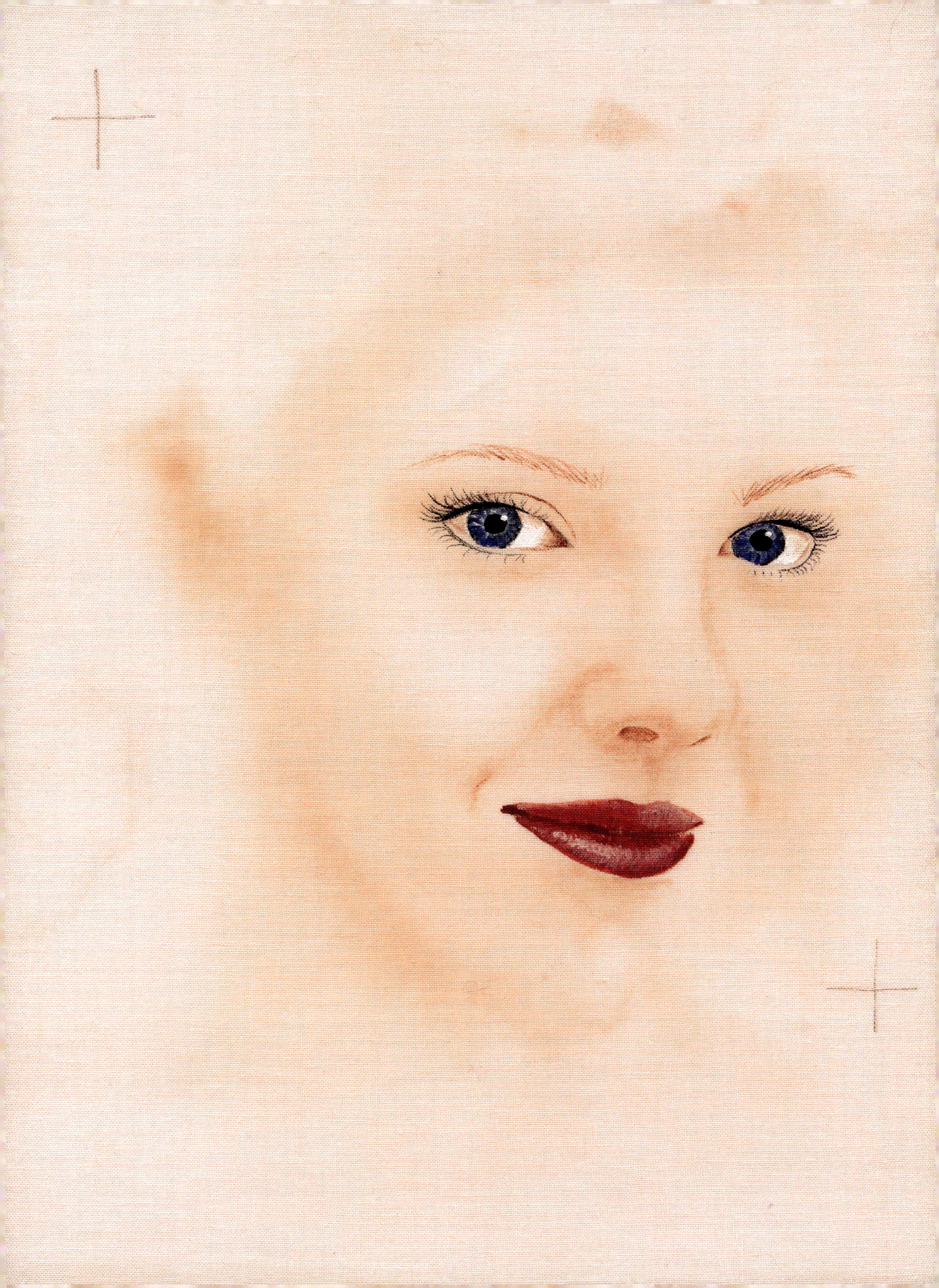

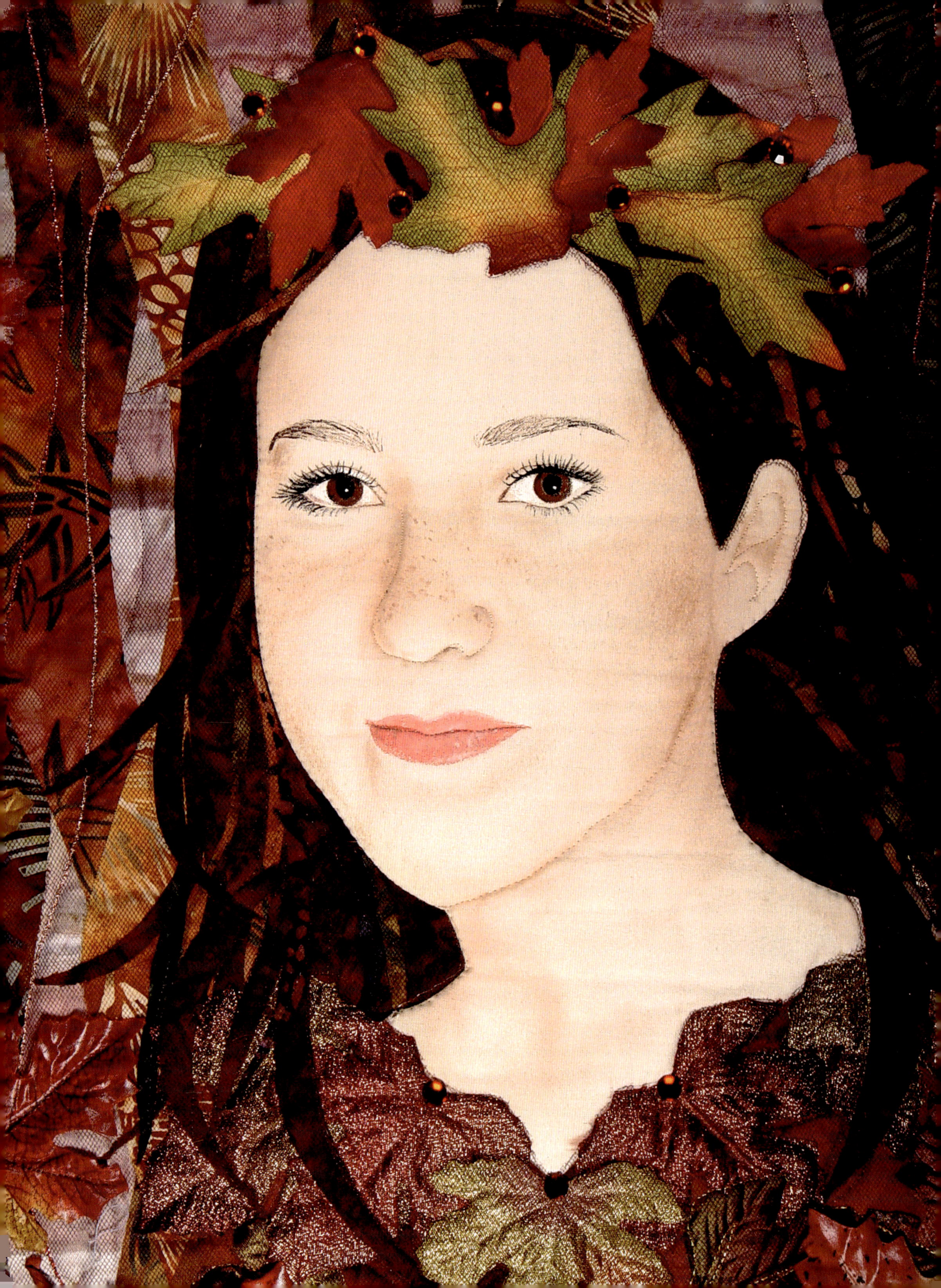

# Freckles, Wrinkles, & Moles

**Freckles, Wrinkles & Moles**

**Paint Colors:**
- DSS41 Burnt Sienna

**Brushes:**
- size 4 or 5 round brush

Every face is different. Freckles, wrinkles, and moles give each person a unique face. It is important to add these features to make the painting look like the person being painted. At the same time, we want the person to be shown at their best. Try to minimize the focus on these features by painting them lighter and smaller than they might appear.

Use very watered down Burnt Sienna on dry fabric and a fine liner brush to paint freckles and wrinkles. Lightly touch the brush to the fabric surface. The watered down paint will cause the paint to bleed into the fabric. This will give a softer look to a freckle. Paint a few freckles to give the indication of freckles. You do not need to paint every freckle seen on the face. Take notice where these features are located and paint a few.

Use this same watered down Burnt Sienna on dry fabric to paint a few wrinkles if they are important to the character of the face. You do not need to paint every wrinkle – just a suggestion of wrinkles to add character to the face.

*close-up* **Victorian Shirley** *by Bonnie Lyn McCaffery. Shirley's beauty mark makes this look like Shirley. Full quilt on page 83.*

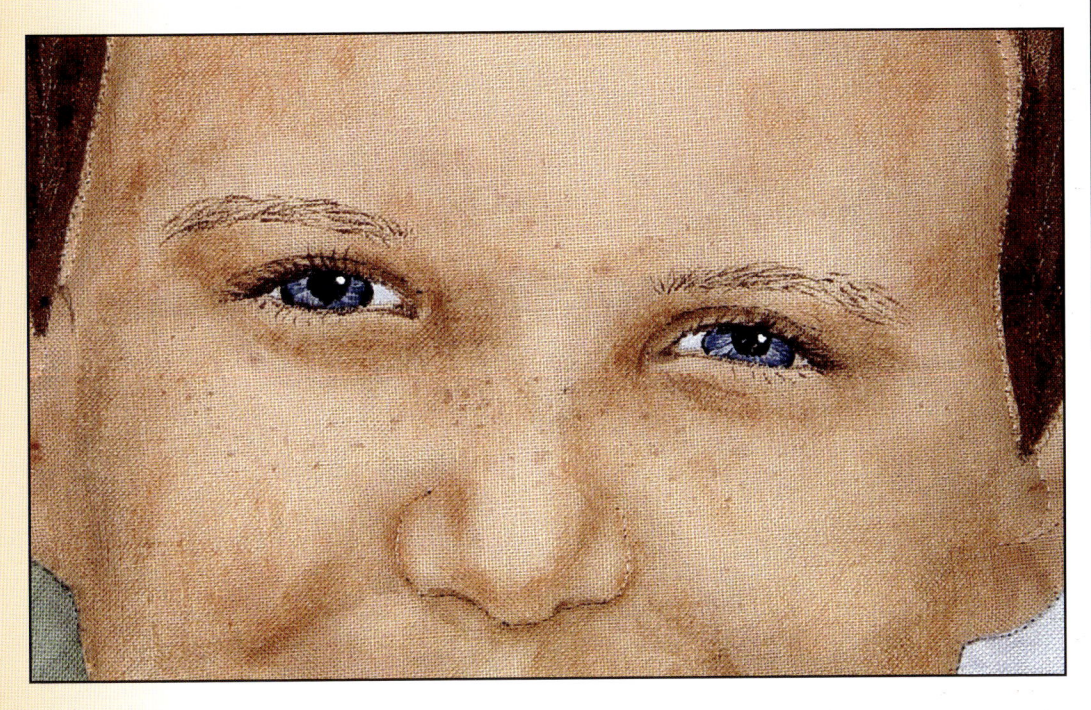

*ABOVE close-up* **The Prisco Boys** *by Bonnie Lyn McCaffery. Dillon Prisco's freckles spot his nose and cheeks. Full quilt on page 46.*

*LEFT close-up* **Autumn** *by Bonnie Lyn McCaffery. Full quilt on page 79.*

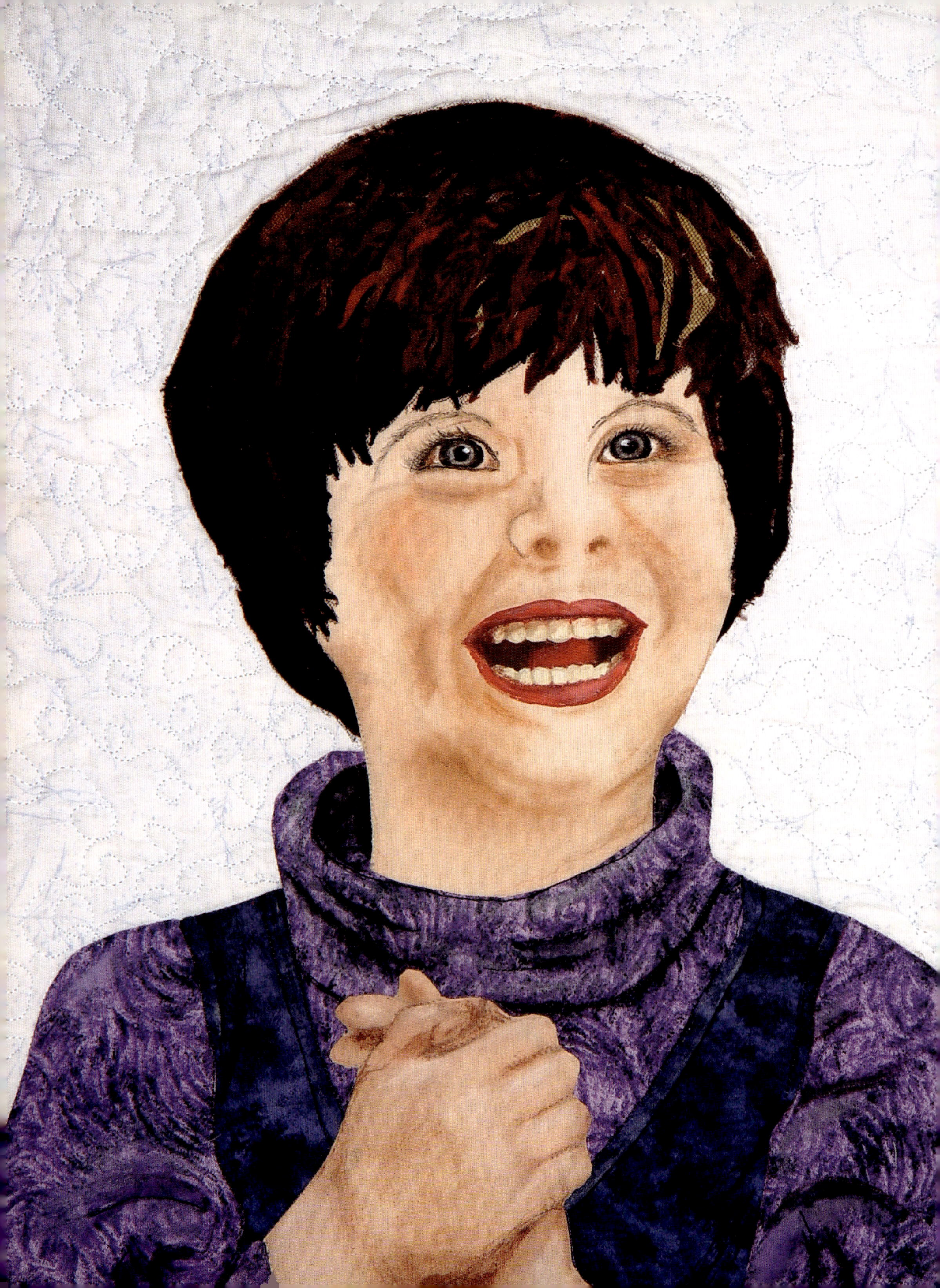

# Teeth

**Paint Colors:**

**Teeth:**
- DSS48 Buttermilk
- DSS 1 White
- DSS41 Burnt Sienna
- DSS13 True Blue
- DAS1 Brush & Blend Extender

**Gums:**
- DSS38 Soft Red
- DSS35 Soft Peach
- DSS41 Burnt Sienna
- DAS1 Brush & Blend Extender

**Brushes:**
- size 0 liner brush for fine lines
- size 4 or 5 round brush for basic colors

Teeth are just slightly more difficult. I recommend painting a closed mouth smiling face to gain confidence and then experiment with painting teeth. Most of the difficulty is because we try to paint what we think we know and not what we are seeing. If your photo has teeth in it, you may want to paint this first (after doing the wet-on-wet shading). This way, if the teeth don't turn out the way you like, you can start over without having to do all of the features again. Be sure to do all steps before giving up. The teeth will look strange until the lips are added.

**1** Teeth are not really white. Look carefully at the teeth and you will see that they often have a slightly yellowish or tannish cast to them. Base coat the teeth with Buttermilk. If the paint dries too quickly, repaint with a mixture of Extender and paint.

**2** Many of the teeth will be in shadow. Without washing the brush, pick up a tiny bit of Burnt Sienna. Blend this into the Buttermilk on the teeth that are in shadow. There will be areas on some of the back teeth that are in even darker shadow (1). Without washing the brush, pick up a tiny bit of True Blue. Blend this into the base colors in the darkest areas of the teeth (2).

The line between the teeth may or may not be visible (3). If it is, mix a little Burnt Sienna and Buttermilk. Use the fine liner brush to paint the line.

**3** Some of the teeth will have highlights. Look carefully at the photo to see where these highlights are located (4). Paint these with White and lightly blend them into the base colors. Take care not to paint the entire tooth with White unless it appears that way in the photo. The biggest mistake with painting teeth is that we think they are all little rounded rectangles.

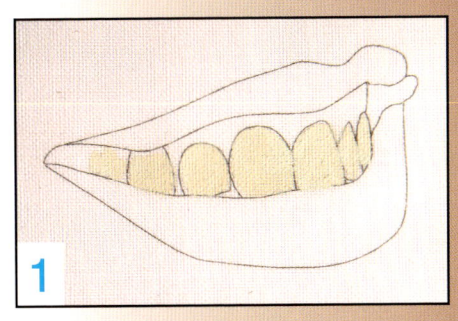

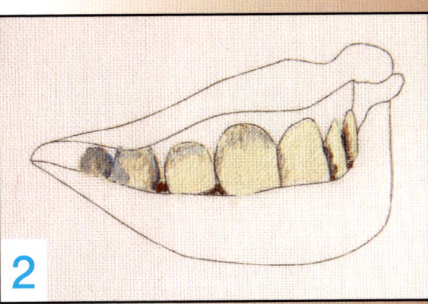

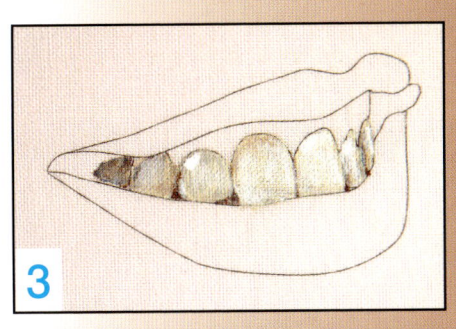

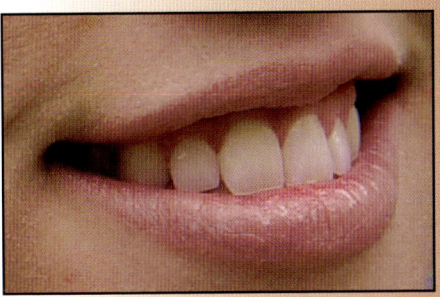

LEFT *Through Kaitlyn's Eyes...Butterflies* by Carol A. Hill. Full quilt on page 78.

**oops!**

**How to Fix It**

It is important to stay within the lines. To make corrections, repaint over top of the mistake. Errors within the lines can just be painted over.

35

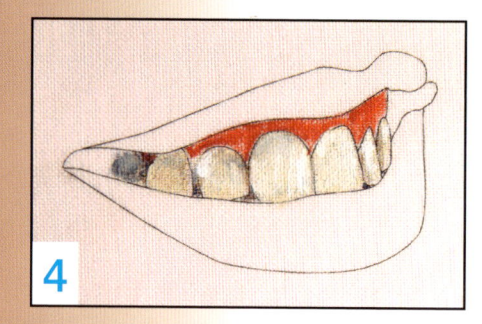

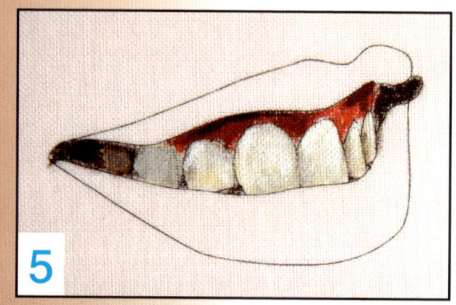

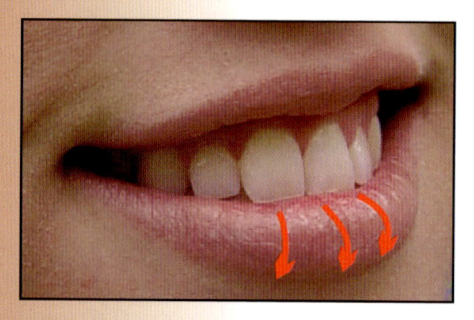

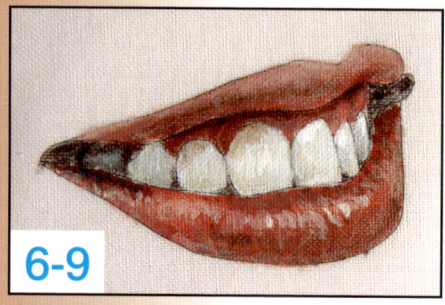

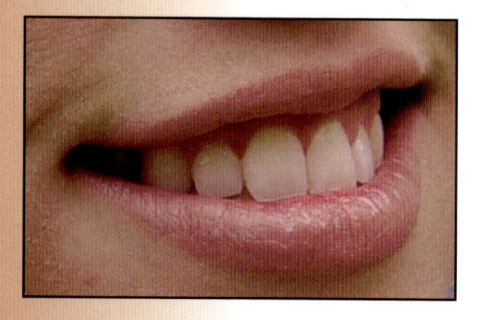

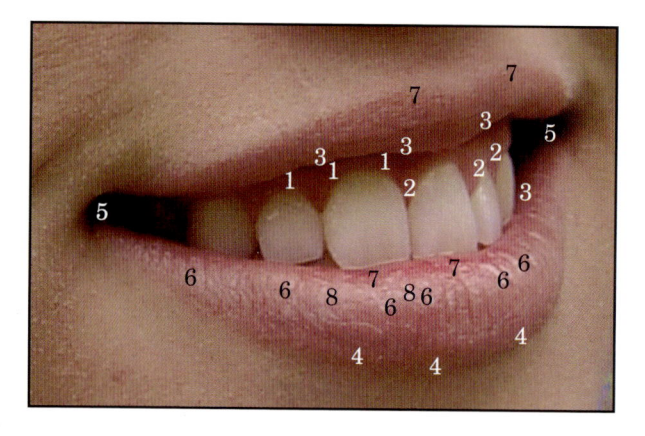

**4** Paint a base coat of Soft Red in the gum area. If it drys too quickly, repaint with a little Extender added to the paint.

**5** Immediately add the shading to the gums under the upper lip (1). Do not let the Soft Red paint dry before adding the shading. Without cleaning the brush, pick up a tiny amount of Burnt Sienna. Add Burnt Sienna to the shaded area in the gums. Blend well. Lighten any areas in the gums as necessary by adding a little Soft Peach (2).

**6** Paint a base coat of Soft Red within the lines of the lips. It is important to stay within the lines, as it is not possible to make corrections. If you paint outside the lines, you will have to make the lips bigger to compensate for the error. If it drys too quickly, repaint with a little Extender added to the paint.

**7** Immediately add the shading to the lips. Do not let the Soft Red paint dry before adding the shading. Without cleaning the brush, pick up a tiny amount of Burnt Sienna. Add Burnt Sienna where the lips come near the teeth (3). Brush a few strokes of Burnt Sienna on the bottom of the lower lip (4). Follow the curve of the lip. Blend the Burnt Sienna into the Soft Red by stroking over it. Notice the dark corners of the mouth (5). Add Burnt Sienna to these places and blend well.

**8** Without cleaning the brush, pick up a little Soft Peach on the tip of the brush. This will be used to add highlights to the lips. Notice the highlights on the full part of the lower lip (6). It runs along the fullness of her lower lip. Brush a few strokes and blend it into the Soft Red. Use curved strokes to help keep the contour of the lower lip. Use a little Soft Peach to soften the top edge of the upper lip (7).

**9** Blend the colors. Use a little less blending to keep the strong highlighted area on the lower lip (8).

NOTE: The color of the lips can be changed by mixing paint colors. Lighten by mixing Soft Peach with the Soft Red before painting the base coat. Men's lips might be better colored by using a mixture of Soft Red, Burnt Sienna, and Soft Peach.

*RIGHT close-up* **Queen of Diamonds** *by Bonnie Lyn McCaffery. The face is Bonnie's own. Full quilt on page 77.*

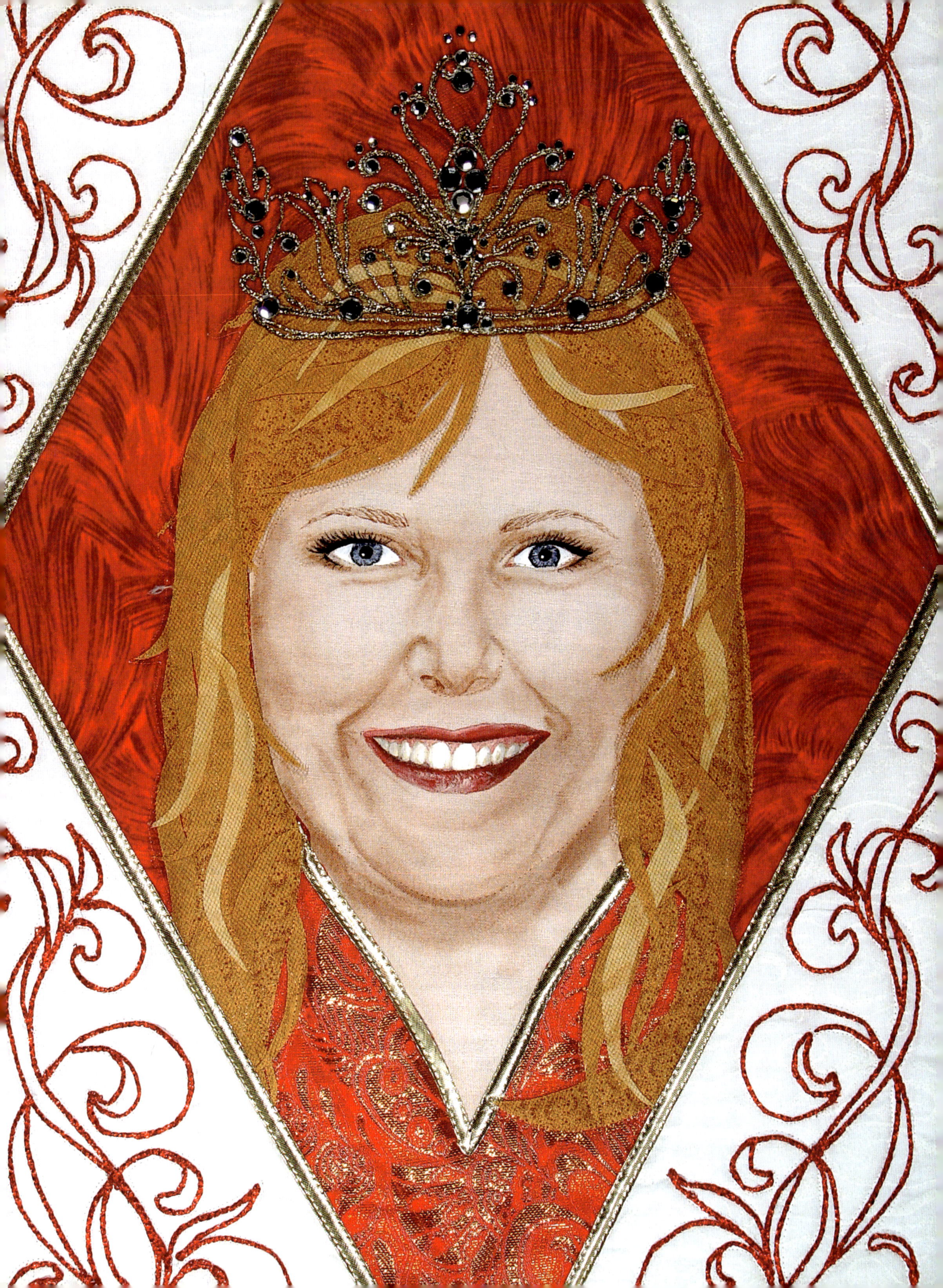

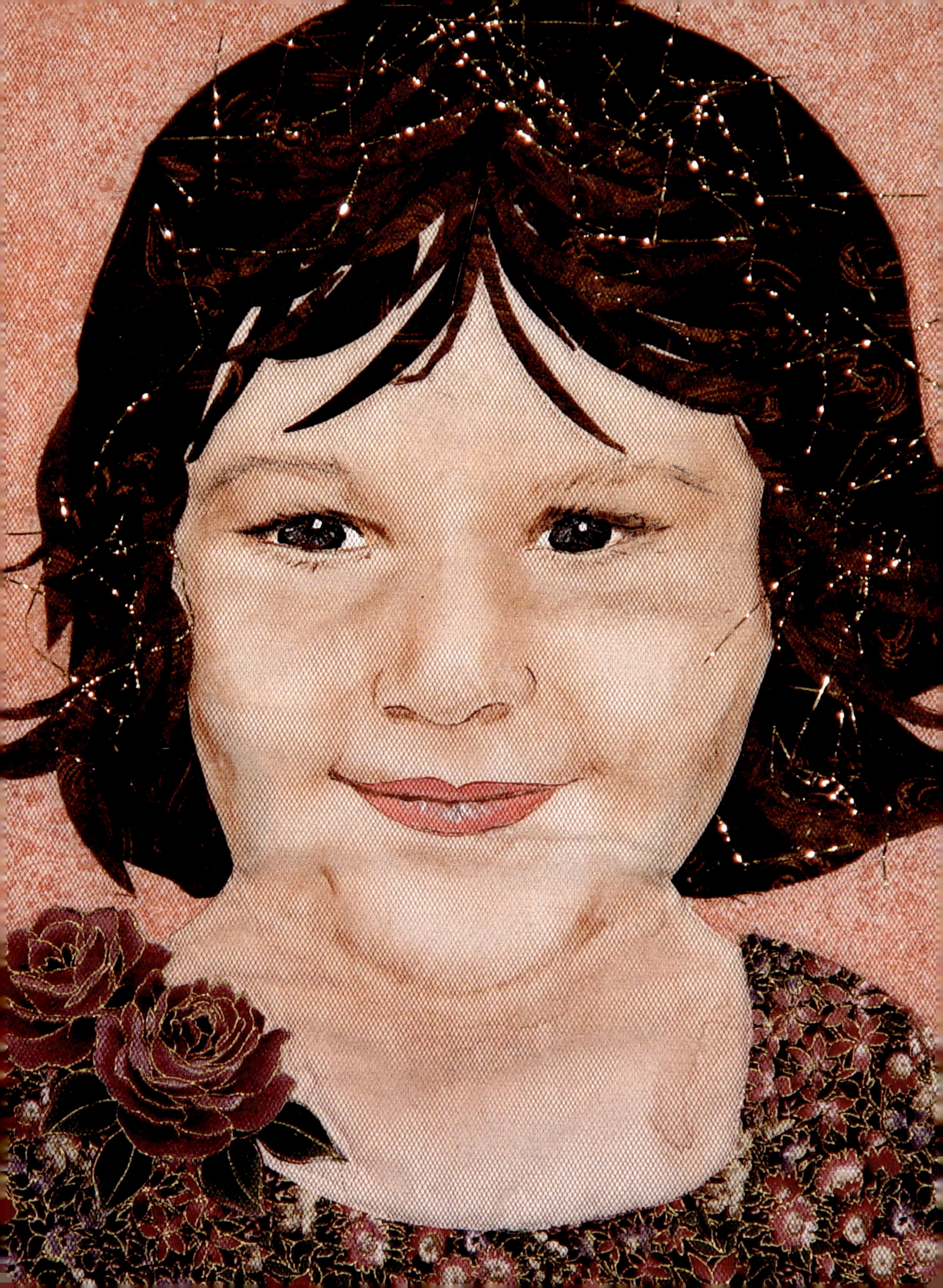

# Painting Men & Children

## Men's Faces

Men's faces have a different complexion. The flesh colored fabric may need to be tanner rather than pink. Look carefully at the photo to select an appropriate fabric color with which to start. The most important thing to remember is to paint what you see. A man's beard area on his face may be darker or grayer, even if he does not have a beard. The lips may be much closer to flesh color than red. Don't be afraid to mix colors to achieve the desired lip color. Burnt Sienna mixed with a touch of Soft Red and Soft Peach may be just what's needed for the color of a man's mouth.

Men's eyelashes are not long and beautiful like a pretty girl's eyelashes. Look carefully to see what they look like. Their eyebrows are usually bushier and often extend into the area above the nose. Your guideline drawing will be the reference you need to determine the location and thickness of the brows.

## Children's Faces

Children's faces tend to be softer. The eyebrow hairs may be lighter, fewer, and thinner. Use the photo and guideline drawing as a reference for the size and thickness of the eyebrow.

Young lips will probably be softer in color. Experiment with mixed colors until they look similar to the photo.

close-up **Albert Becconsall** by Barbara Anderson. Full quilt on page 66.

close-up Dillon in **The Prisco Boys** by Bonnie Lyn McCaffery. Full quilt on page 46.

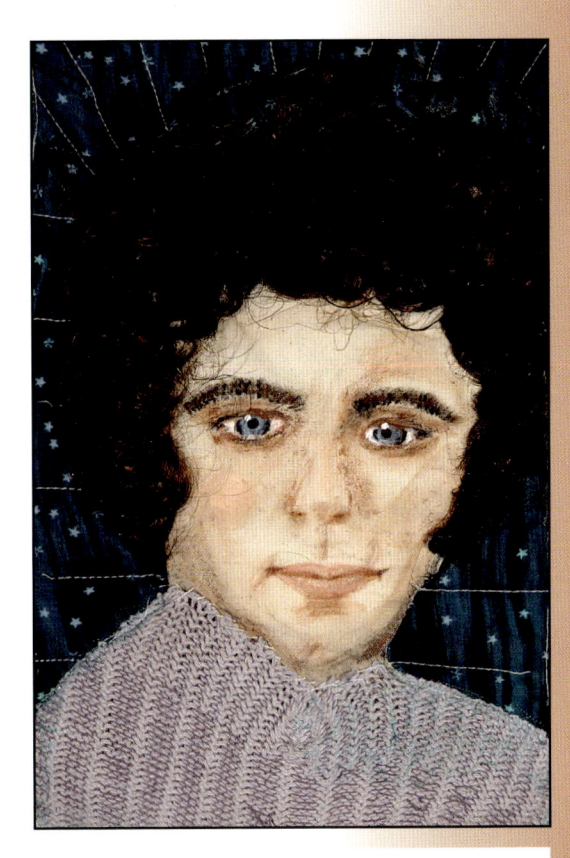

LEFT close-up **Sofia** by Marie Girard, 2003, New Paltz, NY, 20" x 24". The face is Marie's granddaughter Sofia Gallerani Rupert.

close-up **John at 16** by Marion Poplawski. Full quilt on page 67.

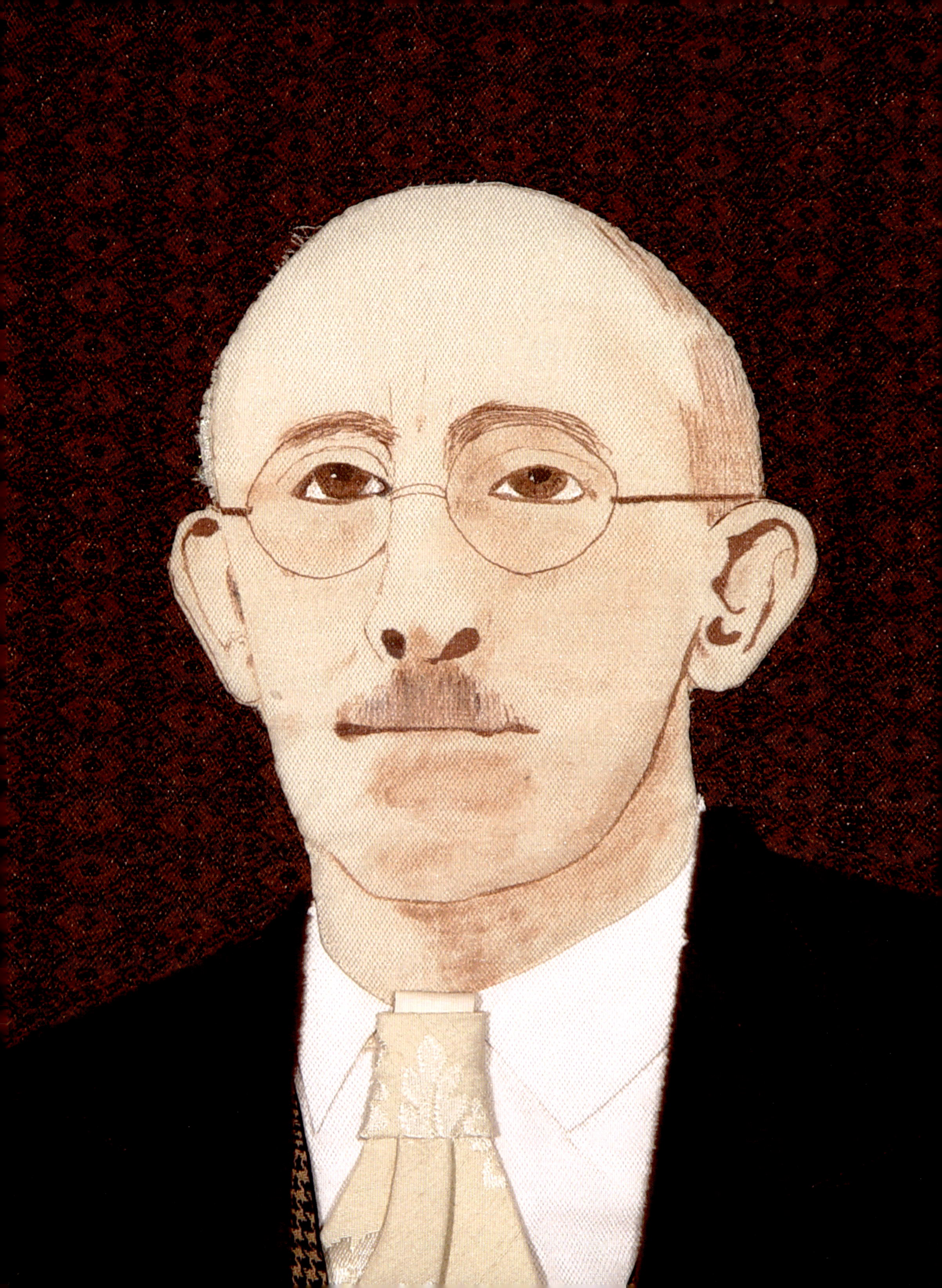

# Eyeglasses

Eyeglasses may be an important feature to create a likeness of the person you are painting. They can be painted with paint or they can be created in fabric or thread. It will depend on the style of glasses.

To paint them, just add them to the guideline drawing. Be sure to add any reflections to the guideline drawing. Paint them after all other features are done. If there is a reflection on the glass in the photo, use a light colored paint to paint it.

Fine metal rimmed glasses are easily created by couching down metallic decorative thread. Use the guideline drawing to trace the eyeglasses on the fabric with a wash-away pen. Use invisible nylon thread and a narrow zigzag stitch to stitch the metallic thread over the line.

Fabric can also be cut in the shape of the glasses. Create a template by tracing the outline from the guideline drawing. Use the template to cut the glasses from the fabric. Position the glasses in place and capture the fabrics under the tulle at the same time the hair is being captured.

If you want the reflective quality of glass in the lens, clear vinyl or plastic can be cut and captured under the tulle.

*LEFT close-up* **Albert Becconsall** *by Barbara Anderson. Full quilt on page 66.*

*close-up* **Abby on the Beach** *by Bonnie Lyn McCaffery. Full quilt on page 44. Sunglasses cut from fabic are captured under tulle.*

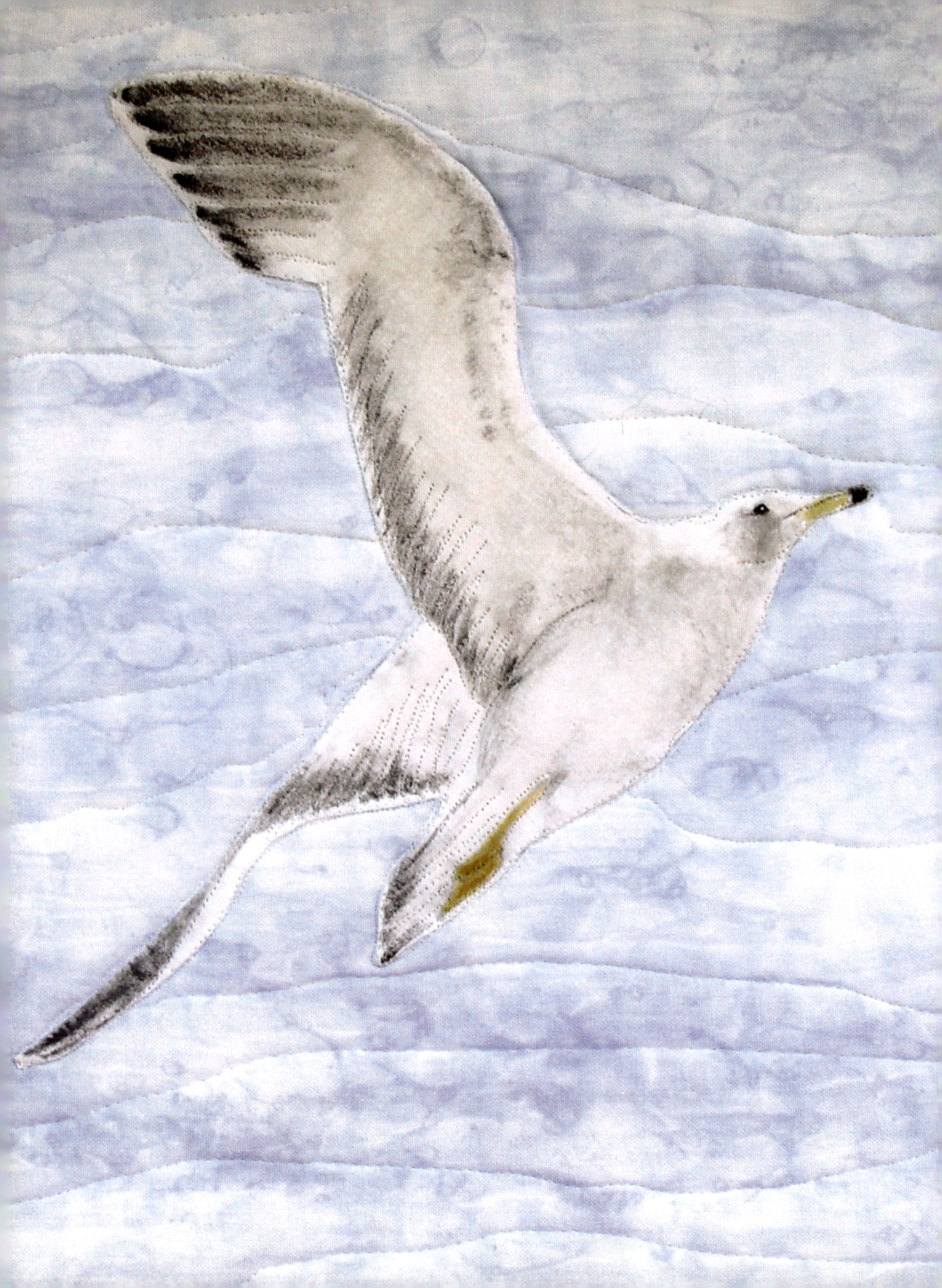

# Painting Other Items

## Hands and Feet

You may choose to do a full body pose. It has been said that painting hands is difficult. Painting hands and feet is no more difficult than painting faces - and you can already see that is easily done. The most important thing to remember is to paint what you see and not what you know.

Enlarge your photo as large as you can. Create a guideline drawing as described on page 14. Enlarge the guideline drawing to the desired size.

You may be able to enlarge the design on the computer and use the "tiled" setting in the printer dialog box. This will put out numerous pages that need to be taped together. A copy center may be able to enlarge sections and print them on 11" x 17" paper.

You can also enlarge just sections, like just the hands or the feet.

Remember to protect the guideline drawing with a plastic report cover, plastic page protector, or some kind of clear plastic.

Paint hands and feet using the wet-on-wet painting technique along with the dry brush shading technique.

## Clothing

Clothing can also be painted. Use the same method of creating a guideline drawing as described above. If the fabric to be painted is dark, it is necessary to use a light table to be able to see the guideline drawing through the fabric.

Abby's jeans were about 30" long. I had to get creative in figuring out how to make a light table. I used an old storm window supported between two tables with a lamp pointed up from below.

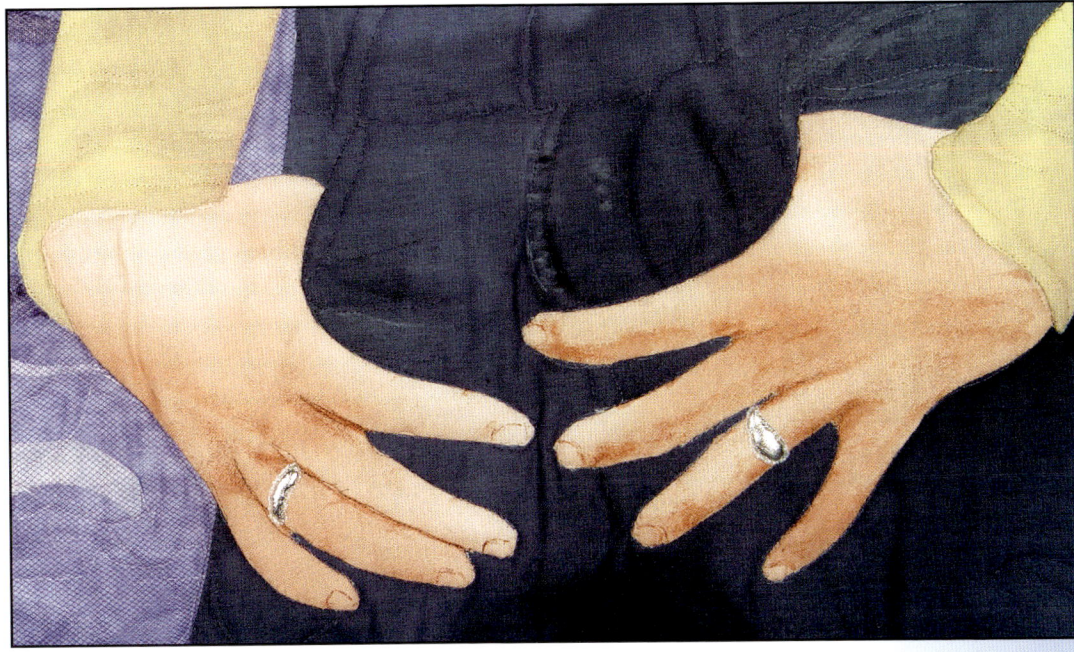

LEFT, ABOVE, & BELOW close-ups **Abby on the Beach** by Bonnie Lyn McCaffery. Full quilt shown on page 44.

**Abby on the Beach** by Bonnie Lyn McCaffery, 2004, Hawley, PA. 68" x 60". The figure on the beach is Bonnie's daughter, Abby (McCaffery) Pittenger. The background, from the ocean line down, is created by capturing cut fabrics and Tintzl under tulle. Abby and the seagulls are painted and appliquéd.

# SECTION III: Designing the Portrait

# Backgrounds

Congratulations! You have done it. You painted a face. Now you will see how to make the painted face into a quilted wall hanging.

## Lining the Face

The painted face is lined with something to help keep the seam allowances from showing through. I like a lightweight fusible interfacing or a very low loft fusible fleece like Pellon Fusible Fleece.

1. Trace the guideline drawing to the fusible side of the lining. It is only necessary to trace the outlines of the head and the eyes. Cut the lining just inside the drawn outline. This will allow for the added width of the flesh fabric rolled over the edge.

2. Lay the painted face with the paint side down on an ironing surface. It is unlikely that the paint will come off on to the ironing surface but, to be on the safe side, lay a clean paper towel on the ironing surface prior to laying down the painted face.

3. Position the cut lining with the fusible side down on the back of the painted face. Carefully position the lining by using the drawn eye outline to line up with the painted eyes. This careful alignment will insure that the face is correctly oriented to the painted features. Iron the lining in place following the manufacturer's directions.

4. Cut the face fabric a scant ¼" beyond the cut edge of the lining. Clip the inside curved areas to the lining fabric. This will make it easier to create a smooth curve. Use a temporary fabric glue stick to glue under the ¼" seam allowance.

## Background

1. Cut a background piece of fabric to the desired size. A fat quarter is a good size to start with. Cut a piece of tear-away stabilizer the same size as the background. Iron the background fabric and stabilizer so they will lay flat. There are some stabilizers that cannot be ironed. Check the label before ironing. The purpose of the ironing is only that it lay flat, not that it is fusible.

2. Lay the background fabric on the stabilizer. Position this on a hard table surface, as you will be pinning the layers together later. It can be positioned horizontally or vertically.

**The Prisco Boys** by Bonnie Lyn McCaffery, 2003, Hawley, PA, 21" x 24". The faces are Nick and Dillon Prisco, Bonnie's nephews. Their names are written in the background with gold metallic paint and the sports balls are rubber stamped on the border.

## Creative Background Choices

A plain or printed piece of fabric serves nicely as a background for the painted face. Some other possibilities might be a busy printed fabric, a pieced background, a painted scene on fabric, or a playful piece of "Fantasy Fabric". Keep in mind while painting or decorating the background fabric that your person is going to cover up some of the background fabric. You do not want to spend a great deal of time decorating an area in the background only to find that it will be covered up. Create a paper template of the person and pin this to the background as a reminder of placement (1).

## Painted Fabric Background

There are a variety of textile paints on the market. Experiment and see which ones work the way you like. The DecoArt SoSoft Fabric Paints can be watered down or painted directly from the bottle and they do not need to be heat set.

The background fabric can be painted in an abstract painterly fashion using the paint straight from the bottle. It can also be watered down and applied to a wet fabric. As you found while painting the face, the watered down paints will blend and flow on the surface, creating a subtle change of color.

A landscape can be painted on the background fabric. Paint the sky with a watered down blue. Dab in some billowy clouds with white and playfully stroke in some trees. It does not have to be a realistic painting. Think of it more as an impressionistic view. An inspiration photo of a scene is helpful for ideas of the design and placement.

Patterns, stripes, and writing can be included on the background. The "Prisco Boys" (on left) have the names of the two boys written repeatedly on diagonal lines. It gives subtle texture and adds an interesting detail to the quilt.

Rubber stamping is another way to add visual texture to the background. Select stamps that will work with paint on fabric. Do not select finely detailed stamps. Large leaves, sports balls, simple flowers and many other rubber stamp designs are available. Rubber stamps were used on the border of the "Prisco Boys" quilt (on left).

I like to use a foam brush to brush the paint on the rubber stamp and stamp on the fabric. Be careful not to put too much paint on the rubber stamp or it will not stamp properly. It is always a good idea to test on a scrap of fabric to become comfortable with the stamping process.

*Helen of Troy* by Deirdre Abbotts, 2003, Westport, CT 24" x 28".

close-up **Autumn** by Bonnie Lyn McCaffery. Full quilt on page 79.

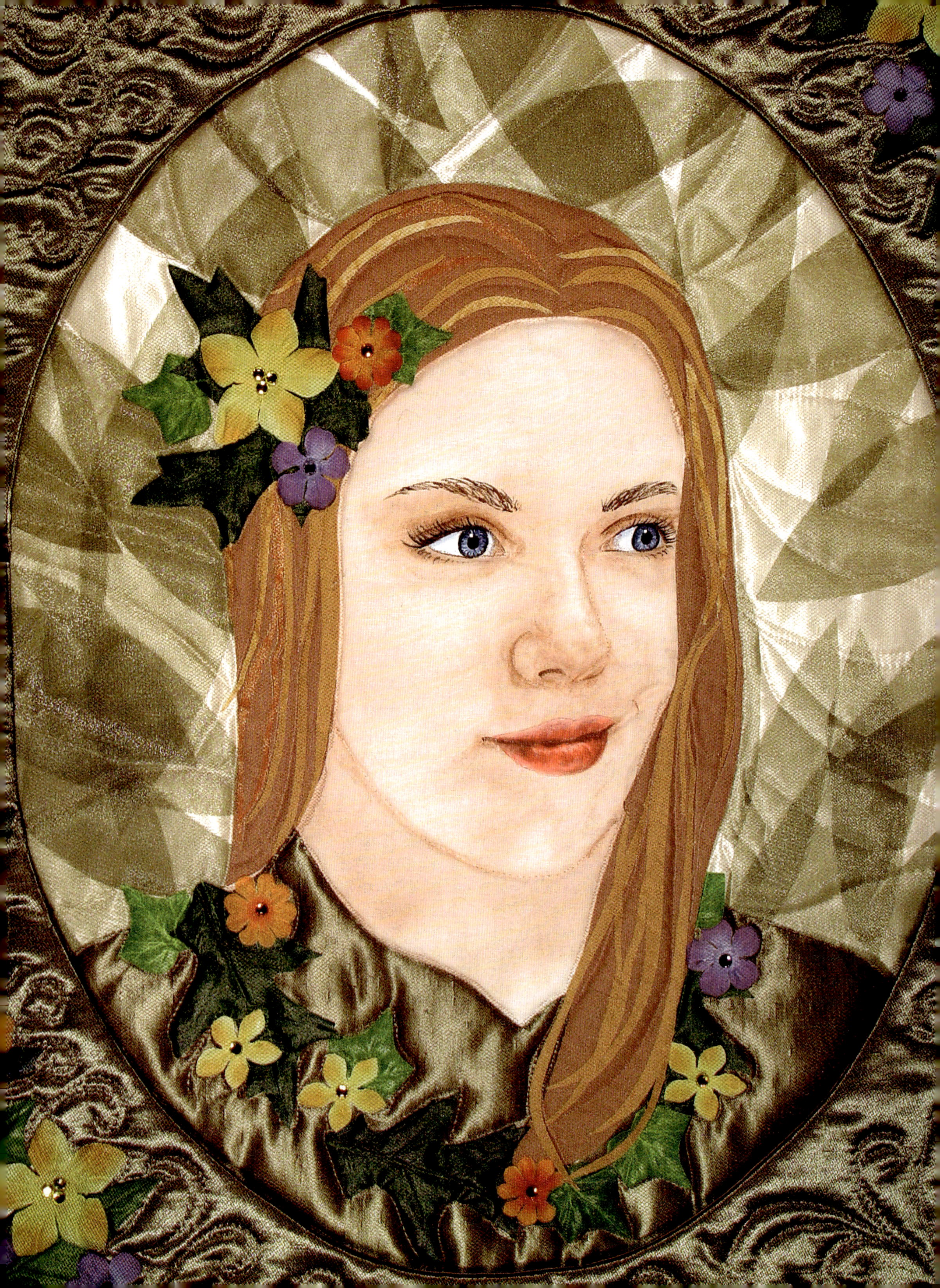

## "Fantasy Fabric" Background

"Fantasy Fabric" is an easy way to add interesting shapes without having to appliqué everything in place. Cut fabrics are layered on the background, covered with a layer of tulle, and then stitched with invisible thread. The hair is already going to be covered with a layer of tulle, so it is very easy to extend the area that will be covered with the tulle.

Cut fabrics are just one thing that can be layered under the tulle. Metallic stars, sequins, Tintzl, cut threads, ribbons, and many other items can be captured under the layer of tulle. "Abby on the Beach" has real seashells captured under the layer of tulle (below). Items to be considered should not be too bulky, heavy, or sharp. Bulky items will not allow the tulle to lay flat. Heavy items will pull the surface of the quilt down. Sharp items will cut into the tulle.

Artificial flowers and leaves can also be captured under the layer of tulle. What an easy way to be able to add nature to a landscape background! When using artificial flowers and leaves, remove the petals and leaves from the stems. Get rid of all plastic parts in the flowers and leaves. The plastic stem that is often glued to the back of a leaf must be removed. It is simply a matter of pulling the leaf away from the plastic stem.

If you are going to create interest in the background by using the "Fantasy Fabric" technique, the background designing should be done prior to adding the face. Once the face and clothing have been added, cover the entire surface with a layer of tulle and stitch the layers together with invisible thread. This will be covered in the section on "Layering and Stitching" (page 73 and 74).

close-up **Abby on the Beach** by Bonnie Lyn McCaffery. Full quilt shown on page 44. Cut fabrics and Tintzl are captured under tulle to give the look of the waves and the sparkle of the ocean.

LEFT close-up **Dear Abby** by Bonnie Lyn McCaffery. Cut sheer fabric shapes are captured under tulle to create an interesting textured background. Full quilt on page 80.

close-up **Abby on the Beach** by Bonnie Lyn McCaffery. Full quilt page 44. Seagulls are hand painted and appliquéd to the surface. Cut fabrics and real seashells are captured under tulle.

*Deirdre of the Sorrows* by Deirdre Abbotts, 2004, Westport, CT, 34" x 39".

# Clothing

## Clothing

1. Lay the prepared head on the background. You will notice that she is naked and needs some clothing. Place a piece of tracing paper over her shoulder area. Trace her shoulder curves and continue the line downward to the edge of the background fabric. Create a neckline to the clothing. This will be the pattern for the clothing.

2. Pin the tracing paper clothing pattern to the right side of the fabric selected for the clothing. Add ¼" seam allowances. Cut the clothing with scissors or a rotary cutter.

3. Clip any inward curves. Turn under and glue the seam allowances with a fabric glue stick.

4. Lay the prepared clothing in place over the shoulders.

## Creative Clothing Ideas

A piece of fabric cut into the shape of a piece of clothing is the simplest approach for covering the naked body. There are several other fun possibilities.

If you have a good photograph of the person in clothing that you want to incorporate into the design, create a pattern for the clothing using an enlarged photo as a guide. Painted highlights and shadows can be added to the clothing using the paints. Look carefully at the photograph to determine the colors of the shadows and highlights on the clothing. Carol Hill added wonderful shading to the clothing in her quilt "Through Kaitlyn's Eyes...Butterflies" (shown below).

You can also paint the clothing on plain white fabric. Deirdre Abbotts painted the clothing for both of her quilts "Deirdre of the Sorrows" (on left) and "Helen of Troy" (page 85).

**Through Kaitlyn's Eyes...Butterflies** by Carol A. Hill. Full quilt on page 78. Beautiful clothing detail painted on printed fabric.

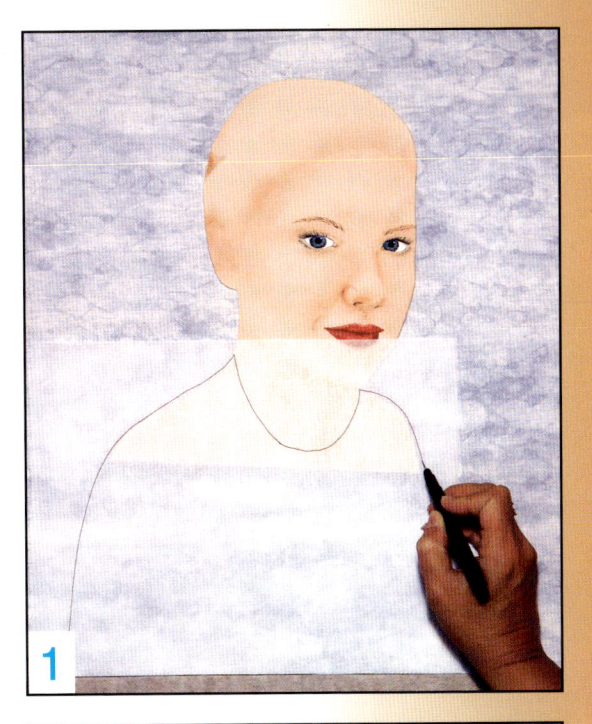

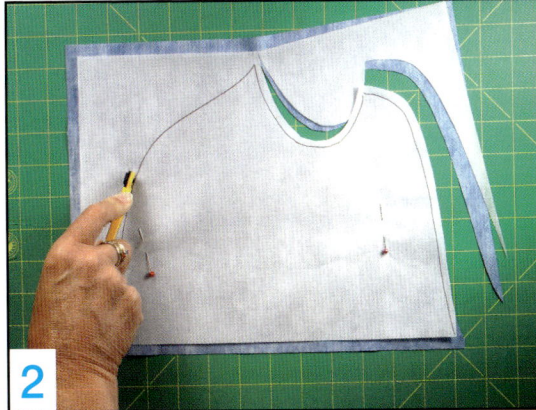

**Carly on the Nile** by Marie B. DiGerlando, 2003, Springhill, FL, 21" x 24". Tintzl and sequin trim are captured under the tulle to add a majestic sparkle to her hair.

The clothing and background are going to determine the personality of the person featured in the quilt. Think about how you want this person to be portrayed. Students all paint the same face, but they all end up with different personalities. Barbara Staskowski gave her girl a very collegiate personality with a tailored blazer in "Princess M" (shown below), while Diann Becker gave the Basic Beauty a party girl personality (shown below), ready for a night on the town. Each quilt will have its own story.

The setting will also tell the story. She can be set in a time back in history as in Kathy Isaacks' quilt "Elizabeth T. Wannabee" (shown at right) or Kathy Porycki's quilt "Kaitlyn's Holiday" (page 62). Kathy Porycki added lace, trim, buttons, and a pin to her old fashioned girl. They both used clothing to give the feeling that these ladies are from the past. Marion Poplawski set her lady on a tropical island with a seashell necklace and parrots in the trees (page 54).

**Elizabeth T. Wannabee** by Kathleen J. Isaacks, 2004, Matamoras, PA, 30" x 30". Feathers under tulle set this girl back in time.

**Princess M** by Barbara Staskowski, 2003, Dingman's Ferry, PA, 22" x 27". A plaid blazer gives this young lady a collegiate appearance.

**Alexa Kay** by Diann E. Becker, 2003, Shohola, PA, 19" x 22". A sassy hairdo and strapless dress give her a party girl appearance. Cut fabric and metallic threads under tulle add texture to the hair.

53

Marie DiGerlando gave her lovely lady an Egyptian personality in her "Carly on the Nile" (page 52). Tintzl and a sequin trim are used to create the Egyptian headdress.

Sandra Brenzel set her painted face in an underwater scene (shown at left). She carefully cut fish, starfish, and plant life from novelty print fabrics. There is no need to worry about the cut edge of the fabric, as it will be captured under the tulle. The Tintzl adds the sparkle to the water. This is where you can have creative fun adding cut fabrics, artificial flowers, and feathers under the layer of tulle.

**Mermaid Fantasea** by Sandra Brenzel, 2004, Barnegat, NJ, 35" x 27". Cut fabrics and Tintzl are captured under tulle to give the illusion of being under the sea.

**Julie Gallagher** by JoAnne Finnigan, 2003, Dingman's Ferry, PA, 22" x 25". The bride is JoAnne's daughter Julie Gallagher. Lace and tulle are used to create a free flowing veil.

**Island Girl** by Marion Poplawski, 2003, Hawley, PA, 22" x 25". Flowers, leaves, and parrots cut from fabric set this portrait on a tropical island.

RIGHT **Contemplation IV** by Bonnie Lyn McCaffery, 2003, Hawley, PA, 50" x 66". The figure is Cheri Mackey, a friend of Bonnie's. Cut fabrics are captured under tulle to create the hair, dress, and the stone floor. YLI Silk Ribbon is twisted to create the branches. Artificial leaves are captured under the tulle.

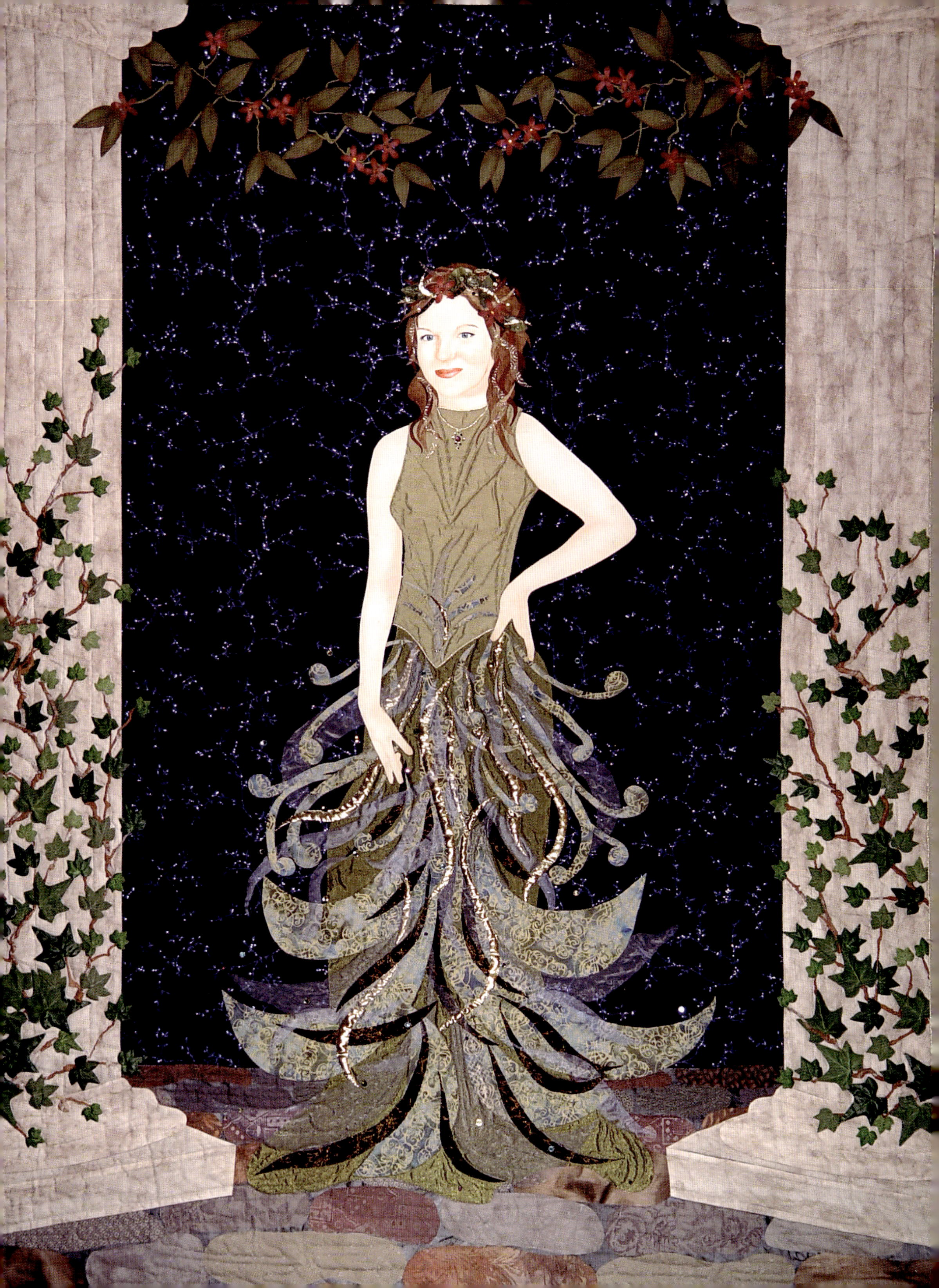

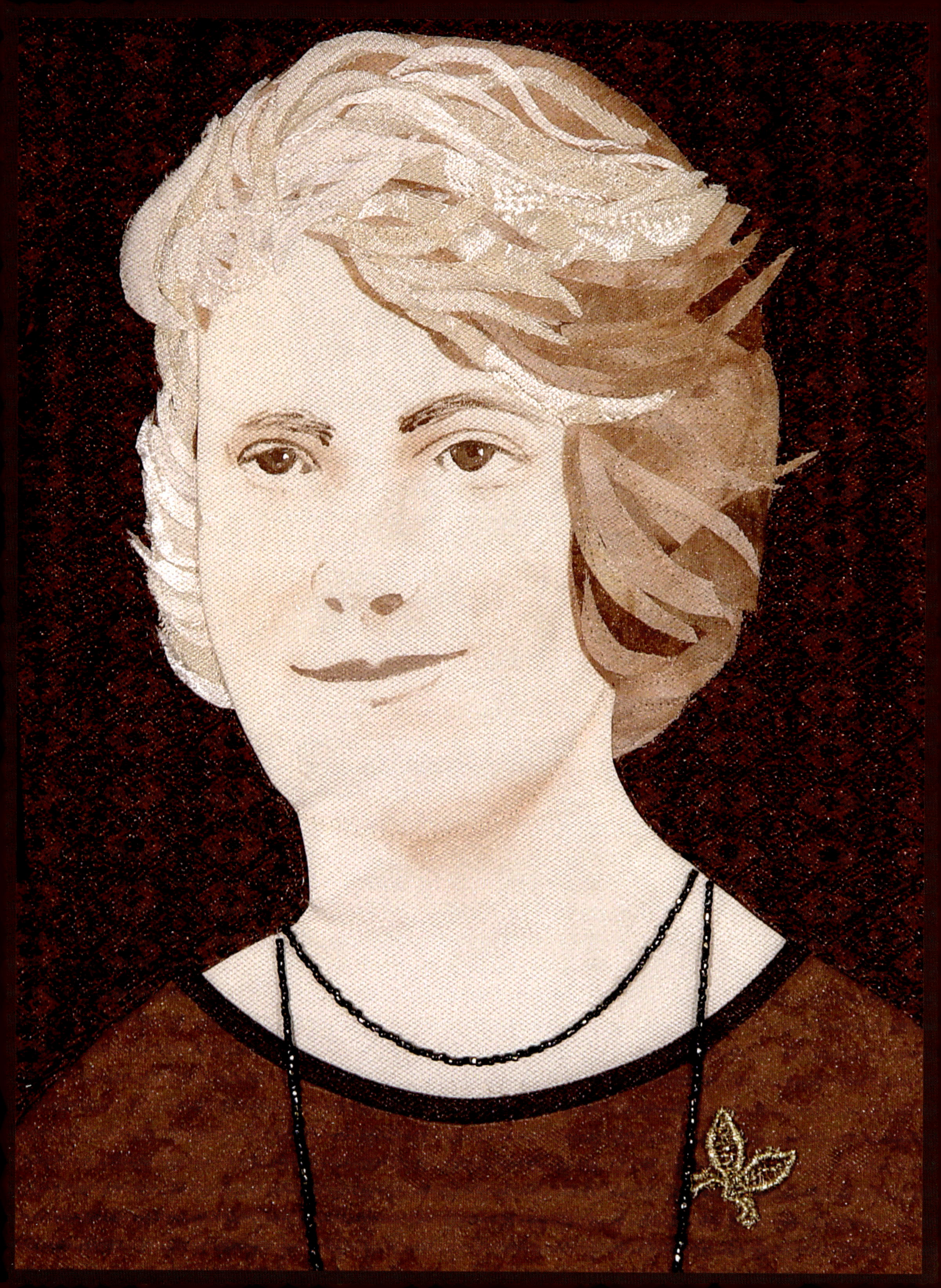

# Hair

## Hair

1. You will need to cover the scull area with a base hair piece. This acts as a solid background for adding hair texture and keeps the scalp from showing through.

   Create a base hair pattern. Lay a piece of tracing paper over your guideline drawing or your reference photograph. Trace the basic shape of the hair. It should be a smooth-lined shape without pieces of hair extending outward. These will be added later. Be sure it is large enough to cover the scull. There is a pattern provided for the "Basic Beauty" on page 90. Trace the pattern on a plain piece of tracing paper or copy paper. Use the base hair pattern to cut the shape from a medium colored hair fabric. Pin this to the right side of the selected base hair fabric and cut on the line. Seam allowances are not necessary for the hair. The edges will be covered with the tulle. Lay the base hair fabric in place on the painted face.

2. A realistic touch to the hair is done by cutting different colored hair fabrics and adding these for texture. Be sure to include fabrics that are lighter and darker than the base hair. It may also be possible to use both sides of the fabrics for variations in hair color.

*Portrait* by Linda Shorten, Hawley, PA, 2004, 25" x 21". Cut fabrics under tulle create a simple flowing hairstyle.

LEFT **Jane (Jennie) Becconsall** by Barbara Anderson. Full quilt shown on page 66. A variety of light, medium, and dark fabrics (cut into slivers) add very realistic highlights, shadows, and texture.

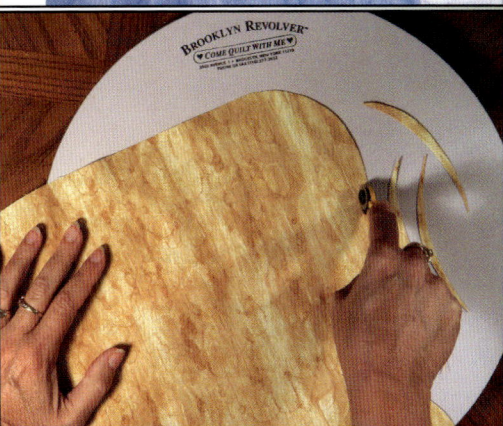

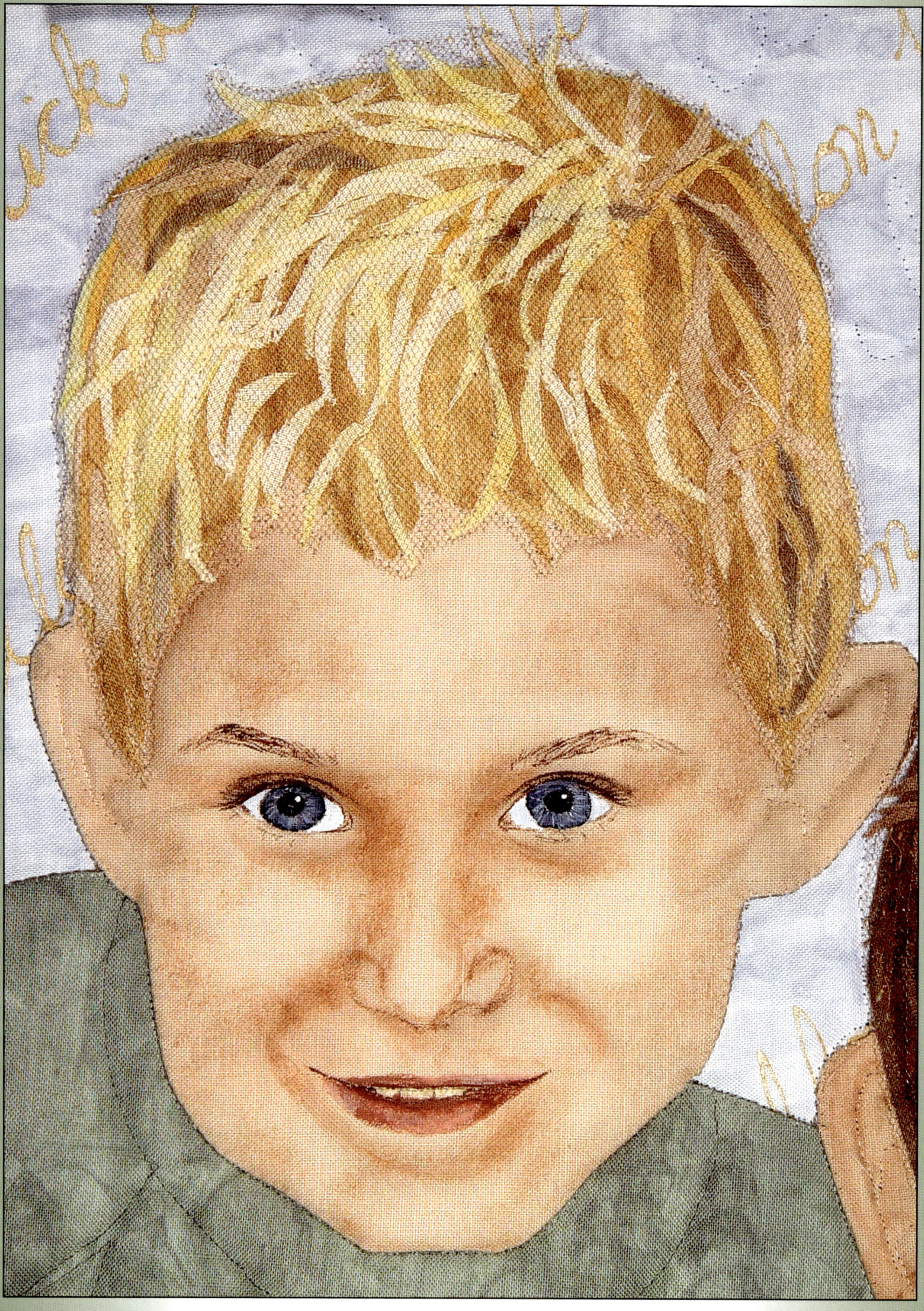

The hair texture pieces can be cut into a number of different shapes. Soft, fat curls create a curly hair texture. Long thin pointed pieces are used for straight hair. Short thin pointed pieces may be the perfect texture for a spiky boys haircut, like Nick's hair shown on the left.

Spray starch the back of the selected hair fabrics. Iron them dry prior to cutting. This keeps the pieces of hair fabric stiffer and easier to handle while positioning them.

Cut the hair texture pieces and position them on the base hair and background. Tweezers are helpful in moving the small pieces. Thread and other creative embellishments can be added under the tulle. Metallic thread adds a sparkle to the hair texture. Allow the thread to fall randomly from the spool.

*LEFT close-up on Nick in **The Prisco Boys** by Bonnie Lyn McCaffery. Full quilt shown on page 46. Small snips of a variety of fabrics create the tossled hair on this little boy.*

*ABOVE **Daydream Believer** by Bonnie Lyn McCaffery, Hawley, PA, 2003, 16" x 22". Wavy cut cottons, metallic sheers, and YLI Kaleidoscope Thread are captured under tulle for the hair.*

59

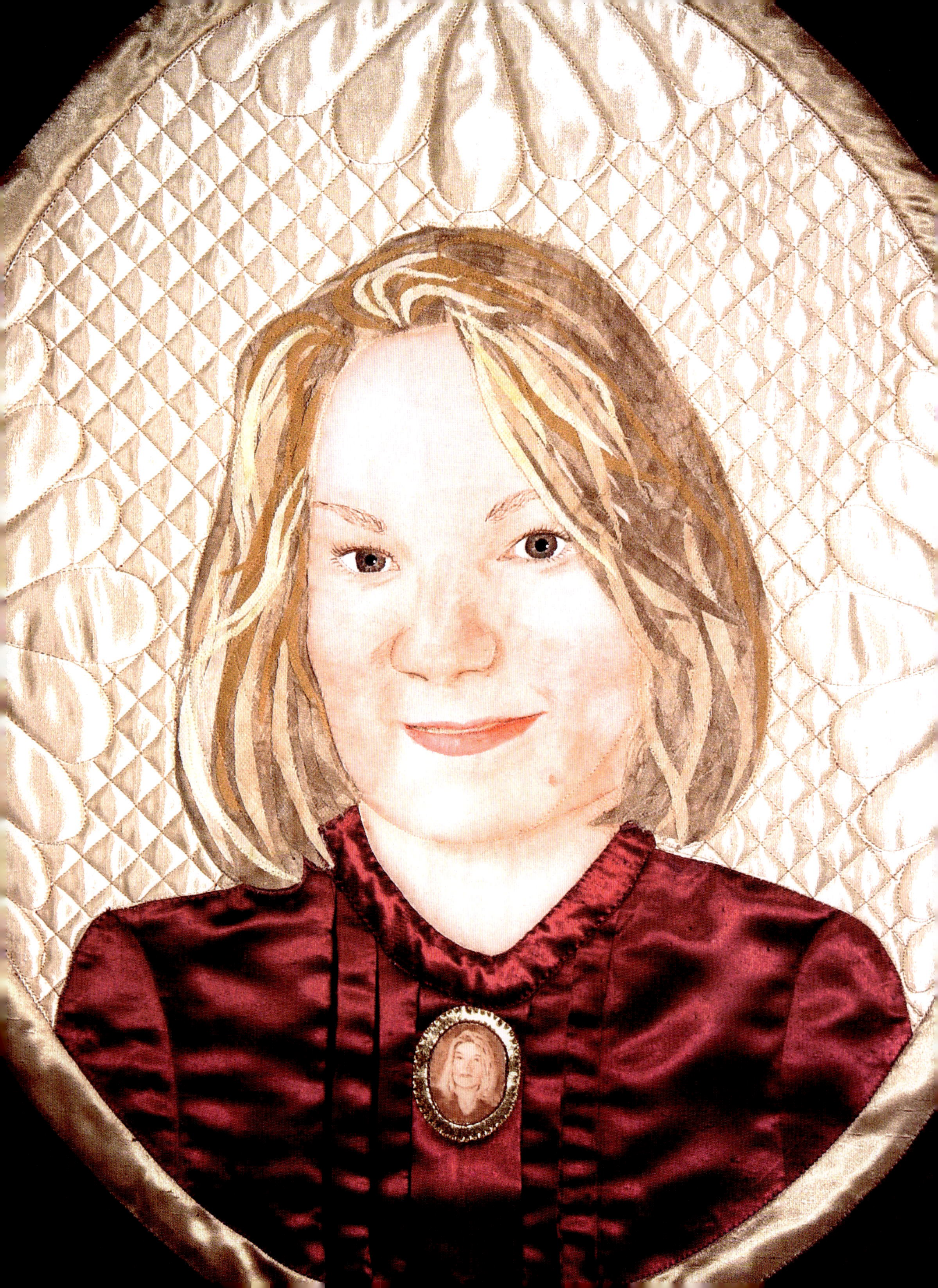

If you want to recreate a hairstyle with more accuracy, create a guideline drawing of the hair on a clear report cover. Outline the areas that are in shadow and highlight. Draw the outline of the face and eyes as a guide for alignment. Use the clear overlay directly on top of the painted face to determine placement of lighter and darker snips of fabric. It is easily flipped up and down to see if the snips of fabric are positioned correctly. Keep the photo nearby as a reference

## Creative Hair Ideas

Doll hair can be added over the base layer of hair. It will take a little playing with, but it is possible to add some realistic hair texture to the design.

Take a look at Mary Murray's "Santa Charlie" (shown below) and Marion Poplawski's "John at 16" (on page 39) and see how they used doll hair for a realistic touch of texture in their pieces.

*LEFT close-up* **Victorian Shirley** *by Bonnie Lyn McCaffery. Full quilt on page 83.*

**Santa Charlie** *by Mary Murray, Milford, PA, 2004, 27" x 28". Artificial holly leaves create a wreath frame around Santa's face. Doll hair under tulle is used for the beard.*

61

One of my students purchased a well-loved doll from a yard sale. She cut the hair from the doll and added it to the portrait of her granddaughter. It was the perfect addition to achieve the wispy look for her granddaughter's hair.

You will be inspired to use all kinds of things for the texture of hair.

Kathy Porycki used a piece of unraveled braided trim for an interesting hair texture on her "Kaitlyn's Holiday" (shown below).

Kathy Krause used painted flower petals to surround her painted face in her "Garden Lights" quilt (shown on the left).

Helen Marinaro created a fabric "do rag" on her painted face quilt on page 84. She dedicates this quilt to her "daughter of her heart" who is a cancer survivor.

**Garden Lights** by Kathy Krause, 2004, Morgan Hill, CA, 26" x 36". Hand painted fabrics are cut and appliquéd in place of hair. Iron-on rhinestones add a sparkly embellishment to the hair.

close-up **Kaitlyn's Holiday** by Kathleen Porycki, 2004, Milford, PA, 24" x 27". Unraveled braid is used for the hair.

**My Scottish Lass** by Bonnie Lyn McCaffery. Full quilt on page 76. The face is Pamela Gardner who lives in Scotland. Long thin snips of fabric create a long straight hairstyle.

**Basic Beauty** by Bonnie Lyn McCaffery. Full quilt on page 92. The face is Bonnie's daughter, Carly (McCaffery) Longhenry. Gentle curl shapes and crescent shapes create a curly hairstyle.

63

**India** by Bonnie Lyn McCaffery, 2002, Hawley, PA, 22" x 25". A real beaded sari is used as a head covering and in the border.

**De Novo** by Michelle Verbeeck, 2004, Dover, PA, 8" x 10". Colorful fabric is used to cover the head.

# Creative Possibilities

## Sepia Tone Portraits

Once you experiment with painting the face, you will find out that it is not nearly as difficult as you initially imagined.

We live in an era when color photographs are a standard, but there was a time when black and white or sepia toned photos were the only thing available.

A sepia toned photograph can be used to paint a color portrait. Enlarge the photo and create your guideline drawing. Use the flesh colored fabric and the paint colors for the eyes, nose, and mouth. You may have to guess at the color of the persons eyes being painted.

A sepia toned portrait can also be made from a color photograph or black and white photo. Make a black and white copy of the photo. Use a light tan fabric as the base for painting. Limit your paint colors to only Burnt Sienna and White. Use a mixture of the Burnt Sienna and White to get a medium value paint. You may also want to add Dark Chocolate (DSS23) for deep dark areas in the painting.

close-up **Victorian Shirley** by Bonnie Lyn McCaffery. Full quilt shown on page 83. This miniature brooch was painted using a magnifying glass and a fine liner brush.

LEFT **Norma Jean** by Bonnie Lyn McCaffery. Full quilt on page 79. The little girl is Bonnie's mom, Norma Jean (Birchall) Giancone, as a child.

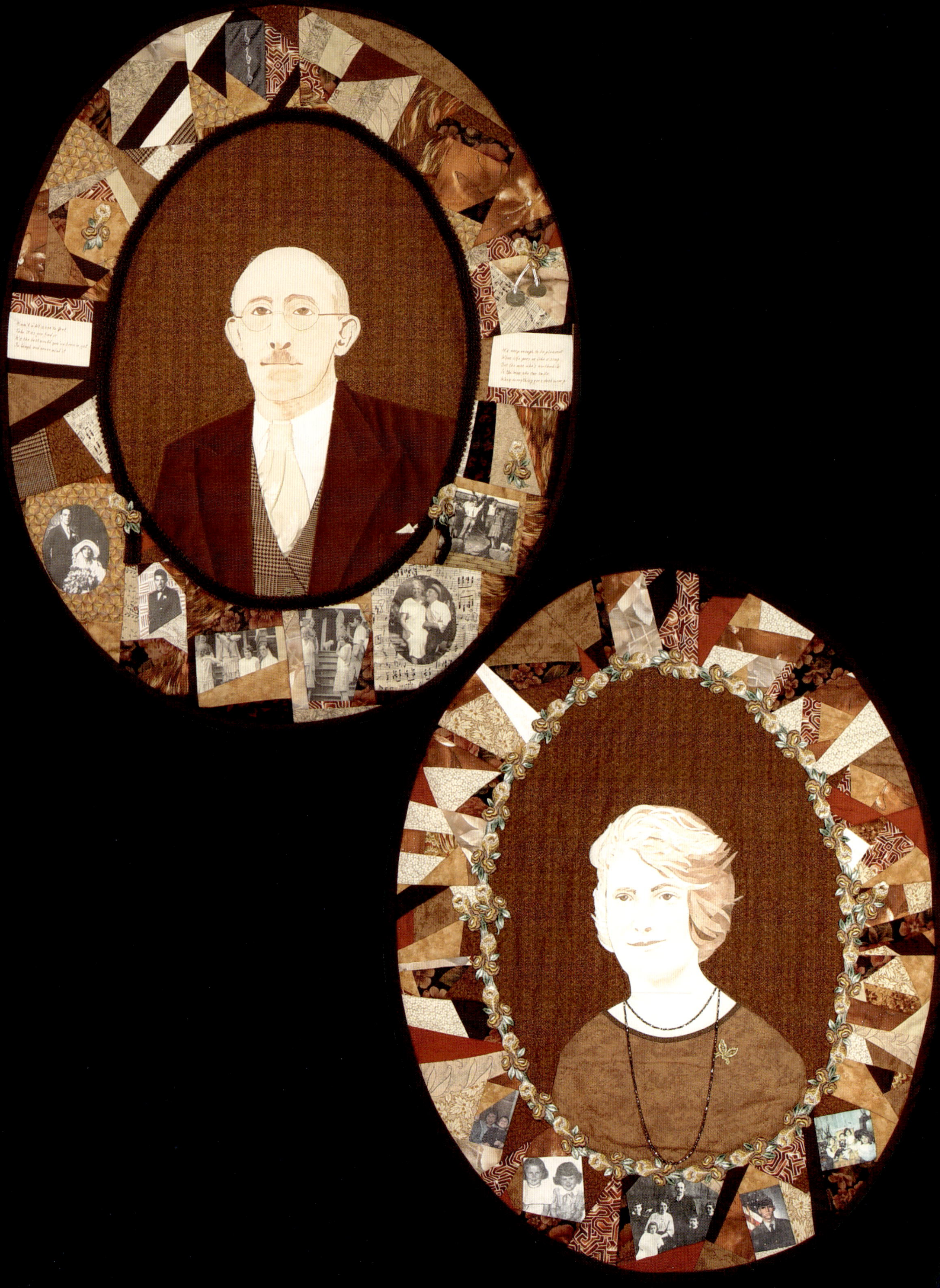

## Miniatures

Throughout the book, almost life size portraits have been discussed. Another creative possibility is to create the portraits in smaller sizes. At some point, the portrait will become so small that it is necessary to forgo using cut fabrics under tulle to do the hair and clothing. These details must be painted.

The brooch in "Victorian Shirley" (page 65) was painted by placing the black and white copy of the photo under the fabric. It was critical to have a good light, a magnifying glass, and a steady hand to be able to paint this miniscule portrait. A light box (that can be turned off and on) is very helpful for seeing the fine details through the fabric.

## Photo Transfers

Photographs, birth certificates, love letters, and handwritten poems will all add a very personal touch to a quilt. These can also be transferred to fabric and incorporated into the design.

Barbara Anderson included family photos into the crazy patch borders of her grandparents portraits (shown on left).

Marion Poplaski added photo transfers of bikes into the borders of her quilt, "John at 16" (below), as a reminder of his joy of the sport.

There are many ways to transfer photographs to fabric. Tee shirt transfer paper will allow you to print an image in color and then iron it on to white cotton fabric. Keep in mind that the image will be reversed once it is ironed on the fabric. Reverse the image before printing it on fabric.

*John At 16* by Marion Poplawski, 2003, Hawley, PA, 26" x 27". Photo transferred bikes and photos are used in the border.

LEFT **Albert Becconsall,** 2002, 27" x 32" and **Jane (Jennie) Becconsall,** 2003, 25" x 32" by Barbara Anderson, Dingman's Ferry, PA. Barbara's grandparents are bordered with a crazy patch border which includes old family photos.

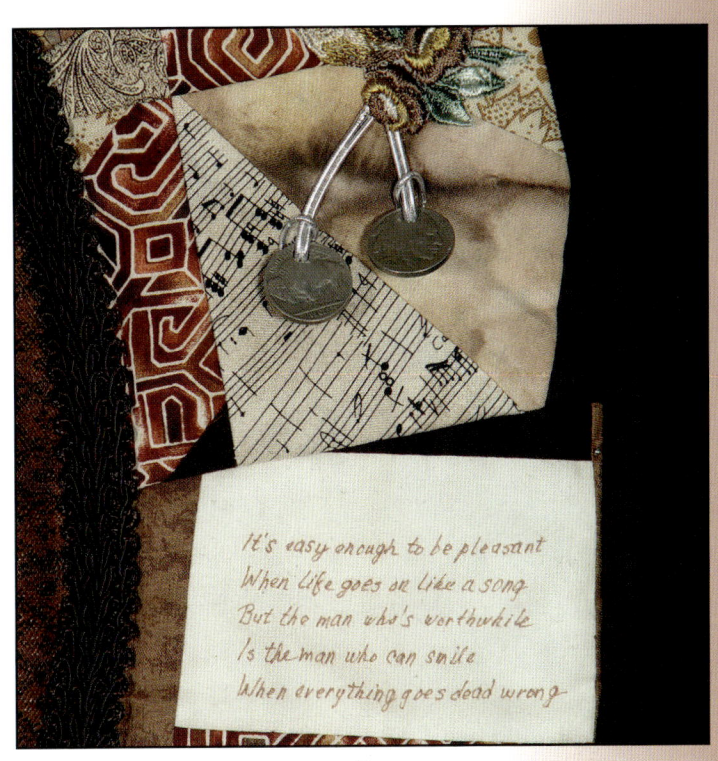

close-up **Albert Becconsall** by Barbara Anderson. Full quilt on page 66. Old coins and a poem often quoted by Barbara's granddad add a personal touch to the border.

67

**Flower Fairy I** by Lynn Page, 2004, Carillon Beach, FL, 55" x 52". *Flowers and butterflies are cut from fabric and stitched to the surface.*

There are prepared fabrics available where you can print directly on to the fabric. These images will not need to be reversed prior to printing. Read the directions and transfer some family photos to fabric. These photos can be incorporated into the border or background. What a lovely family heirloom to have not only a painted portrait of your relative, but also some of the family history as well.

## Captured Items – The "Fantasy Fabric" Way

All kinds of items can be captured under the layer of sheer tulle – just take a look at my Fantasy Fabrics book.

- Cut fabrics – All types of cut fabrics can be captured under the layer of tulle. Randomly cut slivers add texture to the hair or background. Motifs can be cut from novelty fabric to add a very personal touch to the quilt. To cut motifs, spray the back of the fabric with spray starch and iron it dry prior to cutting. This makes cutting easier and helps to hold the fibers together at the cut edge. You must still handle the cut edge very carefully to prevent further fraying.

- Threads and yarns – There is a wide variety of textured threads and yarns available. These add more texture to the hair or background. Just drizzle these on the surface prior to adding the layer of tulle.

*Adam's Yve St. Laurent* by Bonnie Lyn McCaffery, 2002, Hawley, PA, 23" x 19". YLI Silk Ribbon and Candlelight Yarn are captured under tulle along with artificial flowers and leaves. Creative Crystal Iron-On Rhinestones, decorative embroidery, and silk ribbon roses are added after the layers are stitched together.

*Gypsy* by Kathy Oehlmann, 2004, Dingman's Ferry, PA, 28" x 25". Tintzl, ribbons, and dragonflies are captured under the tulle.

- Ribbons – Narrower ribbons can be positioned in the hair to add texture. Position these in the direction that the hair would grow. Ribbon can be tied into bows and added in the hair and on the clothing prior to the addition of the layer of tulle. Silk ribbons captured under the tulle add a whimsical texture to "Adam's Yve St. Laurent" (page 69).

- Metallic sequins, stars, and other shapes – There's a wide variety of metallic shapes available. These will add a sparkly touch to the design. Try to use these sparingly as a little sparkle goes a long way. Take care that punched out sequins and confetti shapes are a single layer.

These shapes are often punched out in a stack and may stick together. Rub them between your fingers to assure that they are singles rather than a stack. Once the layer of tulle is added, stitch right through the Mylar cut shapes to hold them in place.

•Tintzl – I love this stuff. It is similar to Christmas tree tinsel, but it is finer and comes in a beautiful array of colors. Tintzl will add a mysterious sparkle to the hair or the background. Again, use it sparingly as a little sparkle goes a long way. Tintzl is the last item added just before the tulle. If you add it to the surface earlier, it tends to grab other carefully positioned elements and move them around as you are designing. Once captured under the tulle, stitching will hold it in place.

•Artificial flowers (yes, the kind we "decorate" with) – Remove the flowers and leaves from the plastic stems. Get rid of any plastic parts. Once captured under the tulle, you can stitch around or through them to hold them in place. Flowers and leaves can be added to the hair, clothing, or the background. They are a perfect way to set your beauty into an outdoor scene.

*close-up* **Carly Lace** *by Carol A. Hill, 2003, Milford, PA, 26" x 19". Metallic leaves, floral trim, metallic threads, and a lace collar are captured under tulle.*

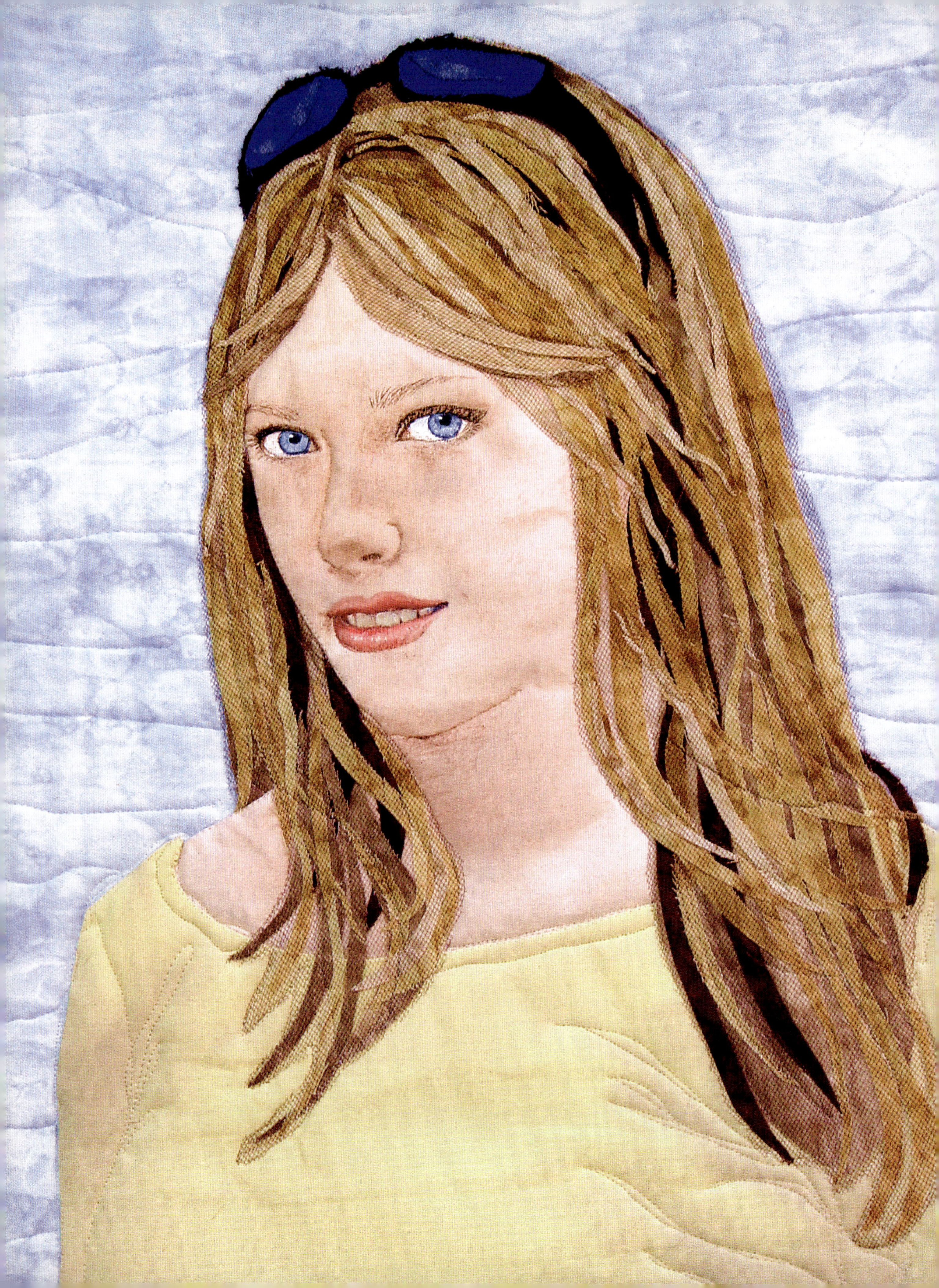

# SECTION IV: Finishing the Portrait
## Layering & Stitching

### Tulle Top Layer

The next step is to cover the surface with a layer of tulle. Tulle comes in a wide variety of colors. The color of the tulle is going to have an effect on the color of the design. Read the section about fabrics on page 8 to decide on the color of the tulle.

1. Cut the tulle a little larger than the background fabric. Iron it flat. Warning: tulle is extremely sensitive to heat. Reduce the temperature of the iron to medium and always test by ironing a corner of the tulle.

2. Examine the evolving portrait to see if there are any other changes to be made. Remove any stray threads or bits of fabric. Anything left on the surface will become a permanent part of the design.

3. Lay the tulle over the prepared design. If possible have someone help you by holding two corners of the tulle while you hold two corners. Hold the tulle about 2" from the surface. When you are both lined up so the whole surface will be covered, lower the corners over the piece.

If you are working alone, you may want to cut the tulle about 3-4" longer. Pull the portrait close to the edge of the table. Hold two corners of the tulle so it is perpendicular to the table. Trap the other two corners of tulle between your legs and the table. Then lower your hands until the design is covered with the tulle.

### Pinning the Layers

4. Pin the layers together with large head pins. The large head pins are easier to see as you are stitching the layers together. Pin as often as necessary to hold the layers together. You will need several pins in the hair area to hold the cut hair pieces in place. You will also need to pin the background area to hold the tulle in place.

If you notice that a cut sliver of hair or other item has moved from the desired location, do not try to reach under the tulle with your hand to move it back into place. This will only cause more things to move. Instead, insert the point of a pin through a hole in the tulle. Use the point of the pin to nudge the misplaced item back into place.

close-up **Daydream Believer** by Bonnie Lyn McCaffery. Full quilt on page 59.

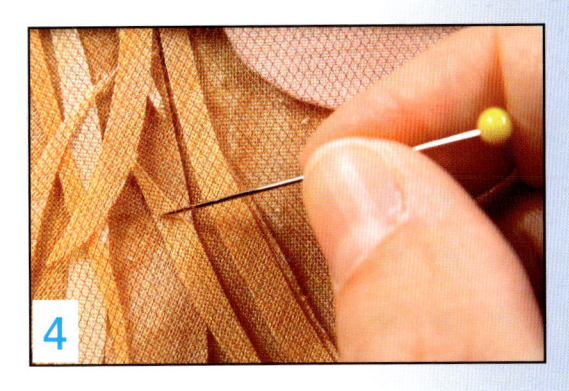

LEFT close-up **Abby on the Beach** by Bonnie Lyn McCaffery. Full quilt on page 44.

73

## Stitching

**5** Thread the sewing machine with invisible thread on top and a neutral colored thread (similar to what will be stitched) in the bobbin. Use a finer sewing machine needle as discussed in the Tools section on page 12. Remember to reduce your sewing machine top tension. Put the free-motion foot on your sewing machine. You are now ready to stitch the layers together.

**6** Read the section on "Free-motion Stitching" (below). Stitch the layers together with free motion stitching and invisible thread. Begin stitching along the outside edge of her hair. Do not stitch right on the edge of the fabric, as it will cause it to fray. Instead, stitch just off the cut edge of the hair. It is necessary to do some free-motion stitching over the textured hair and any other loose items that need to be held in place under the tulle. This will hold the small slivers of fabric in place.

The layer of tulle can be left covering the whole surface of the quilt or it can be cut away from the flesh area and background. If is it left over the whole surface, more stitching is needed in the background area to hold the layers of the fabric together. Do some freeform loops about 2"-3" apart. It should be just enough stitching to hold the layers together. Do not stitch straight around the outside edge as this causes the tulle to pleat and fold. Instead stitch loose curves all the way out to the edge and then back toward the center.

### Free-Motion Stitching

If you are inexperienced with free-motion stitching, this is an excellent opportunity to experiment with it. You will be working with a stabilizer rather than batting and you will also be using invisible thread – so no one will know if you have not achieved perfection.

Most sewing machine manufacturers recommend that you lower the feed dogs. But I would like to encourage you to experiment with the feed dogs left up. It doesn't work with all machines, but it is worth trying. When the feed dogs are lowered, it allows too much sliding motion and you have little control over the stitches. If you leave the feed dogs up however, they grab the fabric each time the needle goes up. The fabric cannot slide around as easily and the stitches are much more controlled. This works very nicely on a Bernina as well as some other machines. It does not work on all machines, so experiment to see if it will work on your machine. If it does not move easily enough, you may need to drop the feed dogs.

Set the sewing machine to a "0" stitch length and "0" stitch width. The speed of your hands and your foot will be the determining factor for the size of the stitches. Start by getting some speed on your foot pedal. This is frightening because we're afraid we will make a mistake. Remember that you have invisible thread, so no one will know if you have not done it perfectly. What happens next is that you think your hands must keep up with your foot speed. You must slow your hands down. They should move in a slow, controlled fashion. The stitches should look the same as if you were stitching 10-12 stitches per inch. "Fast foot – slow hands" is the phrase you should keep in your head as you are stitching.

## Trimming the Tulle

**7** The tulle can be left over the entire surface or it can be trimmed away from the flesh and/or background area. If you leave tulle over the entire surface, you will not need to do the next three steps. Be sure that there is enough stitching to hold the layers together. "Daydream Believer" (on page 59) has tulle over the whole surface.

The tulle can also be left on the hair alone. Nick in "The Prisco Boys" (on page 58) has tulle only over the hair.

**8** If you decide to remove the tulle from the flesh and background, trimming the tulle is done differently in different areas. Along the edge of the hair, cut close to the stitching line. At the areas of the face that have a turned under edge exposed, cut ¼" extra, leaving a flap of tulle over the face.

**9** Tuck this flap of tulle under the turned under edge of the face. Trim away all excess tulle from the background, leaving only the hair covered. "Contemplation IV" (on page 55) has tulle over everthing except the flesh areas.

## Appliquéd Edges

**10** Any areas of the face that have the ¼" turned under edge exposed, need to be appliquéd in place. If the clothing has a ¼" turned under edge and is not covered with tulle, the clothing will also need to be appliquéd in place. Use a blind hemstitch or narrow zigzag stitch and invisible thread to stitch down the edge as described below.

### Machine Applique

Machine applique is a great way to quickly stitch finished edges in place. Baste under the ¼" seam allowance with a temporary fabric glue stick.

Set up the sewing machine bobbin with a thread similar in color to the background. I like to use a neutral colored tan thread if it is a medium colored fabric. YLI Wonder Invisible Thread is loaded on the top of the sewing machine on a vertical spool pin. Reduce the top tension on the sewing machine. Put a 70/10 sharp needle in the machine. Use an open toed foot for easier viewing of the area during stitching.

If your machine has the capability, use a blind hemstitch that has been shortened in length and narrowed in width. The stitch should be wide enough for the "bite" stitch to stitch into the piece being appliquéd. The "straight" stitches should fall only into the background fabric at the edge of the piece being appliquéd. The "bite" stitches should be about 1/16" apart. Move the needle to the center position. Test the stitch on a scrap of fabric – a folded piece of fabric to be appliquéd to a single layer of fabric. If you have not attempted this stitch before you may want to work with a slightly wider stitch. You may need to flip the stitch horizontally so the "bite" stitch will be in the piece being appliquéd and the "straight" stitch is in the background.

If you do not have a blind hemstitch, a narrow zigzag stitch can be used. Shorten the zigzag "bite" stitch to about every 1/16".

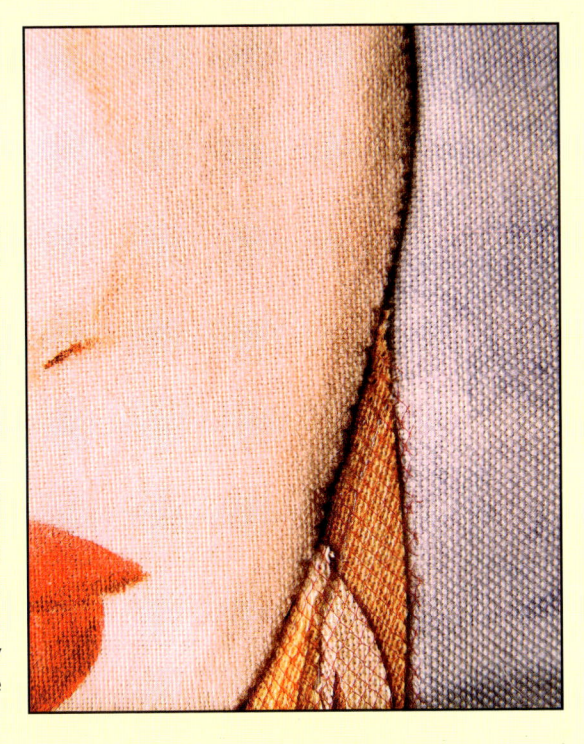

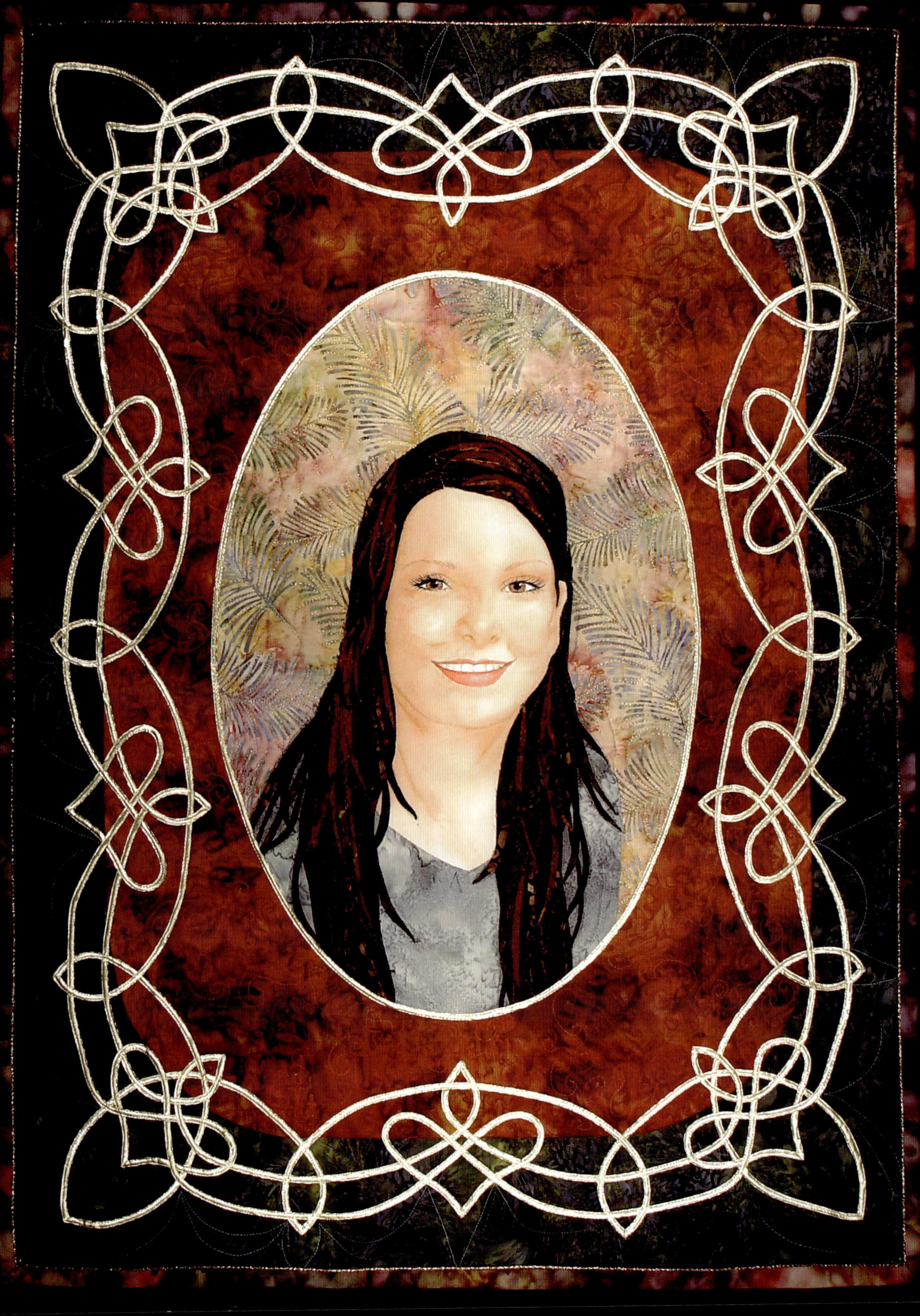

# Borders & Frames

Tear away the stabilizer. It is usually easiest to tear the stabilizer by pulling it against the stitching. This will remove the stabilizer from one side of the stitching and leave the other side looser and able to be pulled up and torn away.

Square up the piece. Keep in mind that the outer ¼" will be in the seam allowance. Cut along the bottom edge with a rotary cutter and ruler. Use this freshly cut edge as a reference to cut the sides perpendicular to the bottom edge. Cut the top edge.

## Simple Borders

1. Measure the central design from side to side across the center of the quilt.
2. Cut two 4" wide border strips using the measurement from step 1 for the length.
3. Pin the top and bottom borders to the central design with right sides together. Stitch using a ¼" seam allowance. Press the seam allowance toward the border. Remember that the tulle is very sensitive to heat.
4. Measure the piece from top to bottom including the added borders.
5. Cut two 4" wide border strips using the measurement from step 4 for the length.
6. Pin the side borders to the design with right sides together. Stitch using a ¼" seam allowance. Press the seam allowance toward the border.

## Easy Accent Borders

A simple way to add a finishing touch to a plain boxed border is to add narrow accent borders. A narrow ½" strip of a bright colored fabric will often add a perfect accent to make your central design stand out.

1. To add the ½" inner fabric border, you will need to cut 1" strips of fabric. Measure the width of the central design and cut two 1" strips the same length.
2. Pin these to the top and bottom of the central design (right sides together) and stitch in place with a ¼" seam allowance. Press the seam allowance toward the border.
3. Measure the design from the top to the bottom, including the top and bottom narrow borders, and cut two 1" strips with this same measurement. Pin these to the side edges of the central design (right sides together) and stitch in place with a ¼" seam allowance. Press the seam allowance to the outer border. Then add the wider borders as described above.

*LEFT **My Scottish Lass** by Bonnie Lyn McCaffery, 2003, Hawley, PA, 25" x 34". The face is Pamela Gardner who lives in Scotland. Clover's Quick Bias forms the Celtic frame.*

***Queen of Diamonds** by Bonnie Lyn McCaffery, 2003, Hawley, PA, 25" x 34". The red binding is accented with gold YLI Candlelight Yarn.*

***Gypsy** by Kathy Oehlmann, 2004, Dingman's Ferry, PA, 28" x 25". A simple narrow border adds an accent to the piece.*

77

## Couched Accent Border

Another way to add an accent border is to couch down a bright, heavier decorative thread along the inner and outer edges of the border.

1. Load invisible thread on the top of the sewing machine and set the machine to a narrow zigzag stitch. The zigzag stitch should be wide enough to capture the decorative thread.

2. Start stitching the decorative thread at a seam line. Leave a 6" tail at the beginning. Stitch around the edge until you are back to where you started stitching. Leave another 6" tail.

3. Use a large eyed needle to thread these tails into the seam without going through to the backing. Bring the needle up about 1" from the seam and cut away the excess thread. The tails should be buried in the batting.

## Crazy Patch Borders

A crazy patch border might be a wonderful way to incorporate clothing or fabric that reminds you of the person in the portrait. There are many novelty fabrics available that cover all kinds of special interests. Use these fabrics to create pieces of fabric that will be used for the borders. It is helpful to cut muslin base fabrics a little larger than the required size for the border. Then add fabrics by placing right sides together and stitching. Flip the fabric open, press, and add more fabrics.

Barbara Anderson included family photos, phrases, and some of Grandpa's old tie fabrics into the crazy patch border on her quilt shown below.

An easy way to do crazy patch is the "Fantasy Fabric" way. Lay the muslin base fabric on a piece of firm tear away stabilizer. Add cut pieces of fabric to cover the muslin base. Cover with a layer of tulle and stitch the layers together with invisible thread. Decorate the edges of the fabric with any of the decorative stitches on your sewing machine. Use this newly created fabric to create your borders.

**Through Kaitlyn's Eyes...Butterflies** by Carol A. Hill, 2003, Milford, PA, 31" x 40". The portrait is Carol's granddaughter, Kaitlyn Curtis. A cut floral fabric is raw edge appliquéd over the border and background.

**Pumpkin** by B.J. Herter, 2003, Milford, PA, 24" x 30". Dimensional flowers are added to the border.

**Albert Becconsall** by Barbara Anderson. Full quilt on page 66.

## Decorative Stitched Borders

A corner accent is a lovely addition to a border. A corner element can be stitched to each of the four corners as a decorative element. Add the borders to the quilt first. The technique I am going to share with you is for bobbin drawing.

1. Trace the corner design on a piece of firm tear away stabilizer.

2. Position the corner tracing on the wrong side of the quilt and pin in place. Take care that the design is centered on the corner.

3. Load the sewing machine with a free motion sewing machine foot. Thread invisible thread in the top of the sewing machine. Wind a heavier decorative thread on the bobbin. I like to use YLI Candlelight Yarn. You may need to adjust the tension screw in the bobbin case to allow the heavier bobbin thread to feed properly.

4. Work with the wrong side of the quilt facing up. To start stitching, first pull the bobbin thread (the heavier thread) to the top (which is really the back of the fabric). Don't forget to lower the presser foot. Then using the Free-Motion Stitching technique described on page 74, stitch around the design following the traced design lines.

5. When you have finished stitching the design, remove the fabric from the machine and leave a 6" tail of the heavier decorative thread. Use a large eyed needle to thread this tail to the back of the fabric and tie off with a knot. Tear away the stabilizer. Do each of the other corners using the same technique.

Digitized machine embroidered corner elements are another creative border accent. Carefully position the fabric and stabilizer in the embroidery unit so the embroidered design is positioned in the corners. Stitch out the design and remove the stabilizer.

RIGHT **Norma Jean** by Bonnie Lyn McCaffery, 2002, Hawley, PA, 18" x 20". The face is Bonnie's mom, Norma Jean (Birchall) Giancone, as a little girl. Bobbin embroidery is done with YLI Candlelight Yarn as corner accents.

RIGHT **Autumn** by Bonnie Lyn McCaffery, 2002, Hawley, PA, 28" x 35". The face is Stephanie Finkelstein. Twisted fabric strips are transformed into branches. Artificial leaves are stitched to the top.

## Oval Template

**1** Fold a standard sized piece of newspaper into quarters. Line up the edges and crease the folds.

**2** You will need to measure your portrait to get an idea of the size of the oval to create. Determine how much of the portrait you want showing. How much space do you want above the top of the head? Place a pin at this point. How much of the clothing do you want to show? Place a pin at the lowest point. Place pins at the sides where you want the design to end. Now measure from the top pin to the bottom pin and then from side to side. Write these numbers down.

**3** Divide the vertical measurement in half. Measure this figure along the longer fold of the newspaper from the center. Mark this measurement on the folded newspaper.

**4** Divide the horizontal measurement in half. Measure this figure along the shorter fold of the newspaper from the center. Mark this point.

**5** From each of the marked points, draw a line parallel to the folded edge of the newspaper until the lines intersect. With a pencil, sketch in a gentle curve between the two lines.

**6** Cut this line through all layers of the newspaper. Save the inner oval section (this will be referred to as the Inner Oval).

**7** Open up the Outer Oval frame. Lay it over the portrait to test the size and shape of the oval. Do not rub the newspaper on the portrait as this may cause some of the newspaper ink to rub off. If the Outer Oval needs to be smaller, fold the paper and use it as a guide to recut a new piece of newspaper. Alter the shape of the curve as you desire. If the oval needs to be larger, fold up the test newspaper Outer Oval and trim away more of the paper. If you have altered the test Outer Oval newspaper, you will need to cut a fresh piece of newspaper using the altered template Outer Oval as a guide. Save the Inner Oval.

**Dear Abby** by Bonnie Lyn McCaffery, 2002, Hawley, PA, 28" x 35". The face is Bonnie's daughter, Abby (McCaffery) Pittenger. An oval frame is very complimentary to portraits. The frame and the portrait are two seperate quilts with a single binding.

## Photo Transfers

Photos can also be incorporated into the borders. Refer to page 67 for instructions to transfer photos to fabric.

## Oval Borders

Ovals are very complimentary to portraits. The technique on the left will allow you to easily create a test template. Experiment until you find a size and shape that works with your portrait. A double page of a standard newspaper is often a perfect size to start with.

### Oval Portraits

1. Use the newspaper Outer Oval frame template for determining the placement of the newspaper Inner Oval template (the center piece that you saved). Lay the paper Outer Oval template frame on the portrait until you are happy with the positioning.

2. Open up the newspaper Inner Oval template and lay it in position within the Outer Oval frame template. Pin the Inner Oval template to the portrait along the cut edge of the oval.

3. Remove the Outer Oval newspaper frame template. Cut ¼" beyond the Inner Oval template.

4. Turn under the ¼" and applique the portrait to the border fabric. Square up the border fabric to the desired size rectangle. Be sure to keep the oval centered.

### Oval Frames

This oval template can also be used to cut out an opening in the border fabric.

1. Position the Inner Oval template centered on the border fabric.

2. Draw around the edge of the Inner Oval template on the border fabric with a temporary marking pen.

3. Remove the Inner Oval template and add ¼" seam allowance to the INSIDE of the oval. Cut the oval from the border fabric.

4. Lay the border fabric over the portrait. The border with the hole cut out of it is easily skewed. Use the Inner Oval template as a guide for smoothing the border into place.

5. Pin the border frame to the portrait. Pin about ¾" from the cut oval edge.

6. Clip the curves. Turn under the ¼" using the temporary drawn line as a guide. Applique the oval using the technique on page 75.

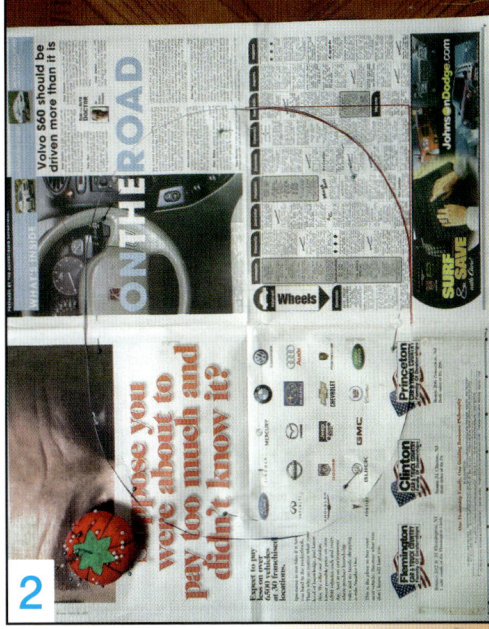

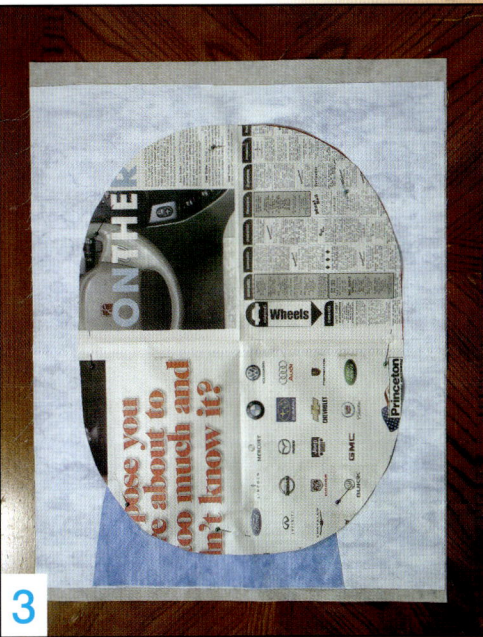

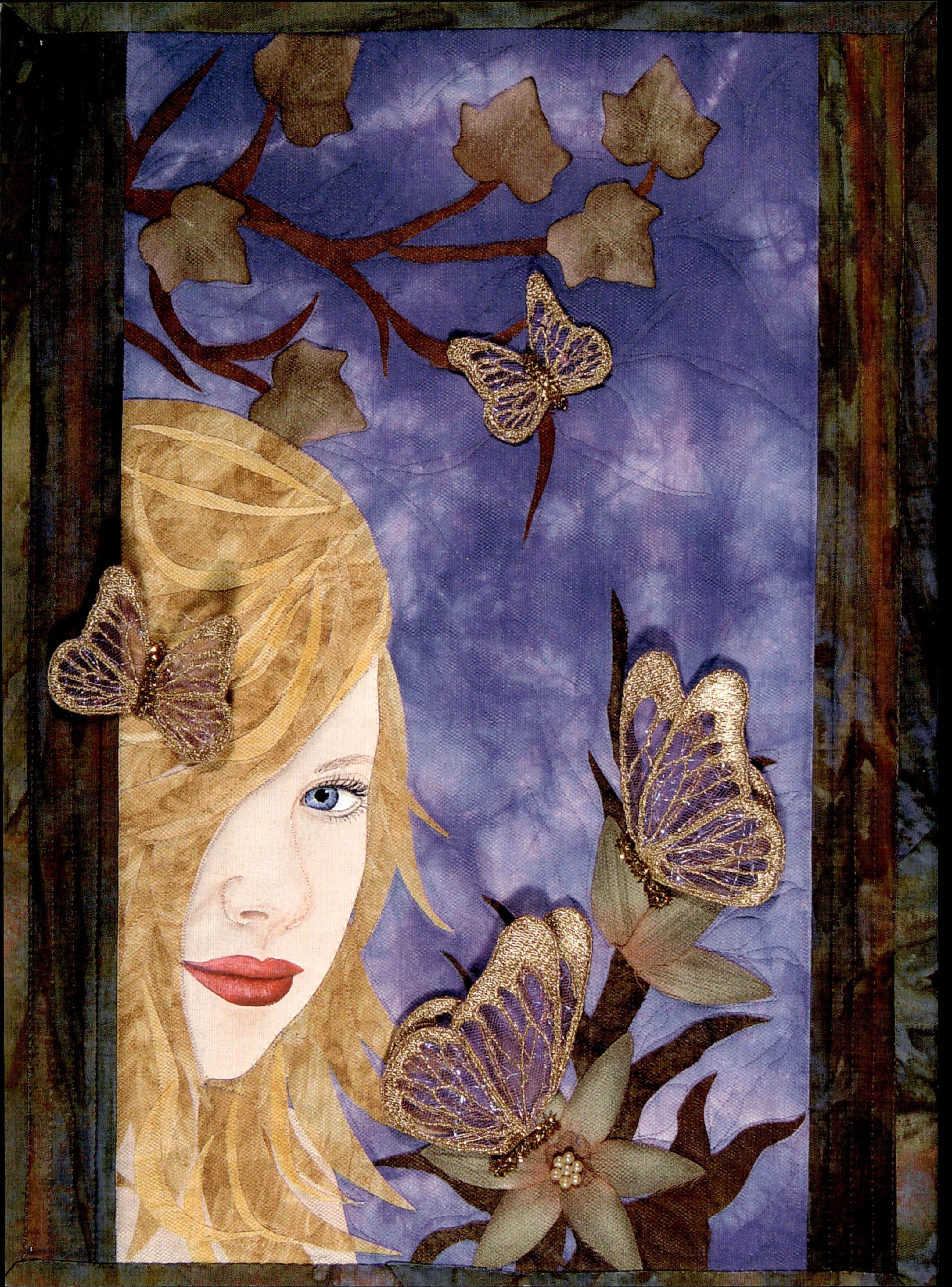

# Finishing Touches

## Quilting

Once the quilt top is complete, layer it with batting and backing. Baste the layers together using thread basting or pin basting. I prefer to baste with large head straight pins on small pieces. You will have to take care that the pins do not catch in the tulle as you are quilting. Baste about every 4" to 6".

I prefer not to have heavy quilting on the flesh areas. Quilt areas on the face that will have natural indentations. The crease of the eyelids, the inside edge of the eye, the curve of the nose and nostrils, the curve of the chin, and the line where the lips come together are all areas where quilting can be added. The natural indentations of fingers, elbows, toes, and any other creases in the flesh can also be quilted.

The hair is quilted with lines in the direction that hair would grow. This helps give a realistic look to the hair.

The background and clothing will also need to be quilted. Think creatively here. If a plain background fabric has been used, the quilt line will be another element of design. It can be straight vertical rows of a repeat design, or an all-over repeat design. Leaves are a natural addition to a landscape or natural background. Stippling, leaves, curly-q's, and any type of design that fills in the background will help depress the background area.

*Caitlin* by Mary P. Murray, 2003, Milford, PA, 20" x 22". Curly quilting lines stitched in red thread enhance the hair texture.

LEFT **Bernina Butterfly Fantasy** by Bonnie Lyn McCaffery, 2003, Hawley, PA, 12" x 17". Embroidered butterflies embellish this portrait.

**Victorian Shirley** by Bonnie Lyn McCaffery, 2004, Hawley, PA, 24" x 27". The face is Shirley Botsford. Heavy quilting with YLI Silk Thread adds a Victorian flavor to this portrait.

83

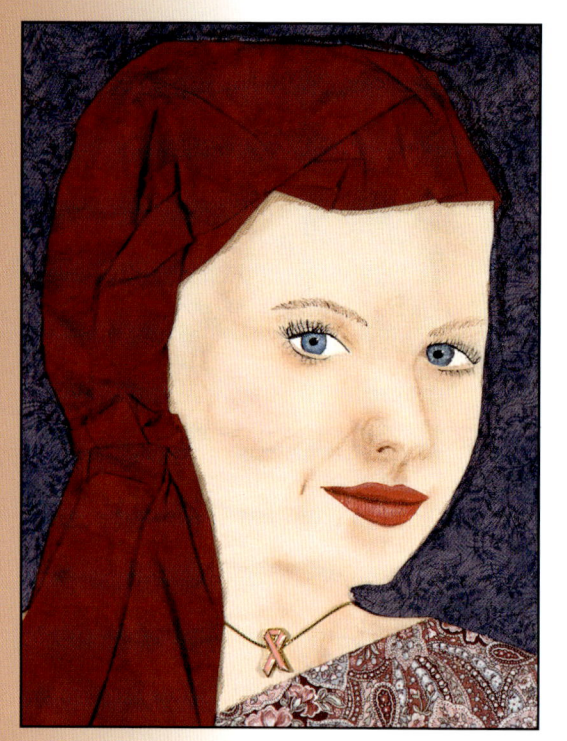

*I Can Do This...I Can Survive* by Helen Marinaro, 2004, Sparrowbush NY, 22" x 27". A common phrase repeated in the class was "I Can Do This". Helen named this quilt for the daughter of her heart, Kim Winners, because she's a breast cancer survivor.

## Embellishments

Any hard or bulky embellishments should be added after the quilting has been done. This way they will not be in the way as you are machine quilting the layers together. Items that are stitched on will need a strong thread similar in color to the item being added. Bury the knot between the layers just as you would if you were hand quilting.

- Buttons and beads – Beads add a lovely sparkle and dimension to the design. They can be added to the hair, background, and clothing. Buttons make a wonderful finishing touch to clothing. Stitch them on using a strong thread.

- Iron-On Rhinestones – I love Creative Crystal Iron-On Rhinestones. These are Swarovski Crystals with a heat sensitive glue on the back of them. Creative Crystals has a tool called a BeJeweller that is used to fuse the rhinestones in place. The crystals can also be fused in place using a mini iron and great care. Remember that the surface is covered with a very heat sensitive fabric – tulle. If the iron is too hot or stays in contact with the tulle for too long (only seconds) it could melt - and then you would have to be creative to come up with a solution to hide the melted tulle.

- Charms and Jewelry – Charms make lovely earrings and necklaces. Take care to select smooth edged charms that will not get caught in the tulle and tear it. Stitch the charm securely in place. Do you have a favorite brooch from your grandmother? What a lovely way to display it on a painted portrait of her. Just pin it to the quilt after the quilt is completely finished. Maybe you have an earring without a match. Remove it from the ear hook or post and stitch it to a single exposed ear. A single earring can also be used as a necklace or hair adornment. Think creatively and you will come up with many other ideas.

*Charlene's Memorial* by Maureen Forseth, 2003, Pine Bush, NY, 12" x 12". Pearls are added as earrings and a necklace.

*Katherine Staskowski* by Barbara Staskowski, 2003, Dingman's Ferry, PA, 20" x 27". The face is Barbara's husband's grandmother. A real necklace is added.

***Helen of Troy*** by Deirdre Abbotts, 2004, Westport, CT, 24" x 27".
Beading adds a wonderful accent to the collar, sleeve, and cuffs.

## Binding and Labeling

Use your favorite method to bind the quilt. The technique I like to use is to add a 2" strip to the back of the quilt. Turn under the edge and roll it to the front of the quilt. This edge is then stitched with invisible thread and a zigzag or narrow blind hem stitch.

## Quilt labels

The final step is to label the quilt. A photo transfer or computer printed fabric label is the perfect way to add a photograph. You could even use the photograph that was used to paint the portrait.

Labeling the quilt is an important part of creating it. Include the information of the maker as well as the name of the person in the portrait.

With computer printing technology, it is quite easy to create a label that can be printed directly on fabric or transferred to fabric. Refer to page 67 for more information. It is nice to include a photo of the person whose portrait has been painted. You could also include other information such as how old the person is if it is a child, where the picture was taken, and any other information that might be interesting in the future.

*Kaitlyn's Holiday* by Kathleen Porycki, 2003, Milford, PA, 24" x 27". Buttons adorn the hat and a brooch accents her blouse. Her hair is made from untwisted cording.

*Quilting Diva* by Bonnie Lyn McCaffery, 2004, Hawley, PA, 22" x 24". Premade beaded fringe trim by Expo International Inc. is draped and stitched to create the scarf so often worn by Karen Boutte (shown in the portrait) who lives in California.

RIGHT close-up *India* by Bonnie Lyn McCaffery. Full quilt on page 64.

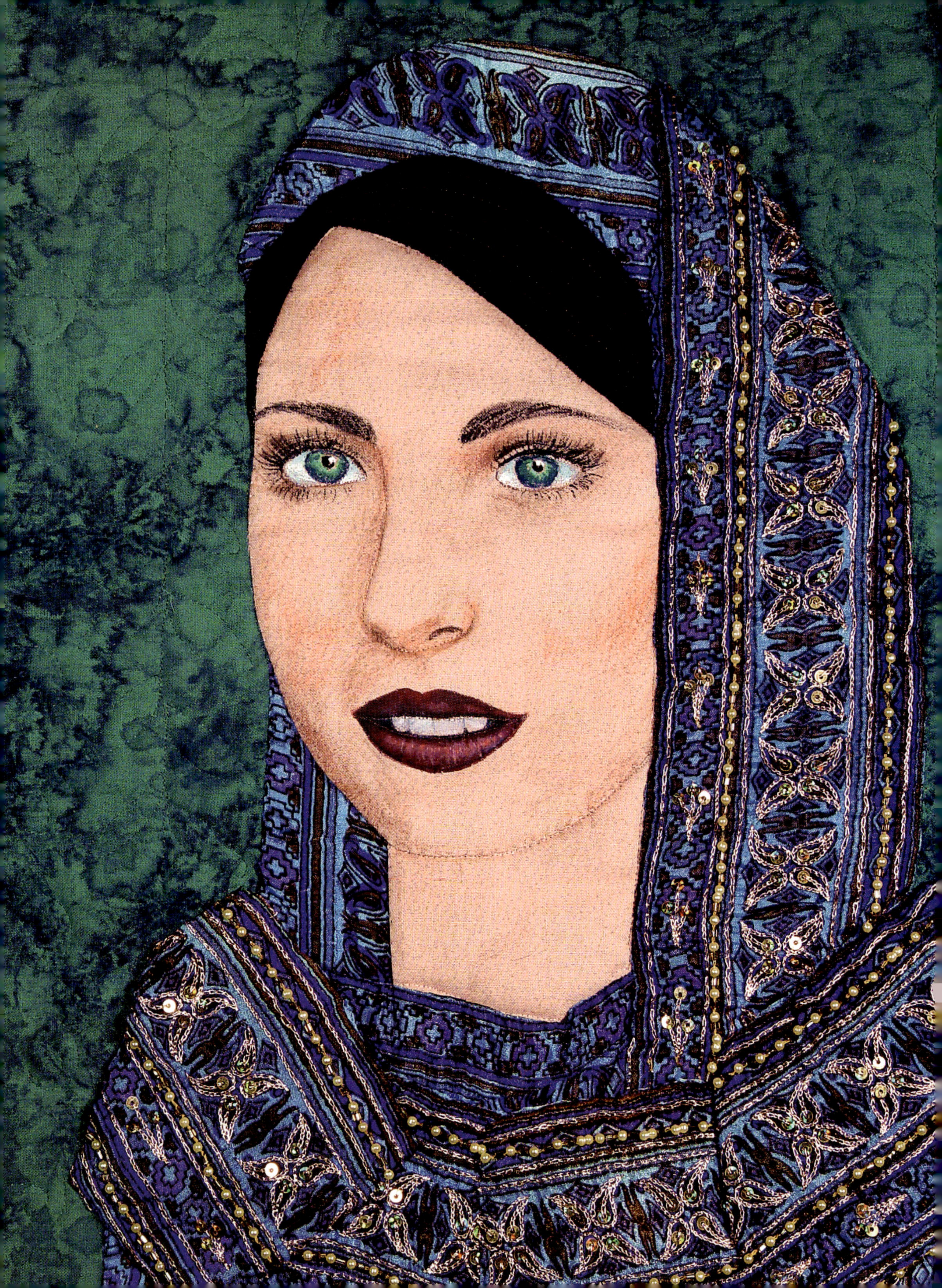

"Basic Beauty" photograph reference

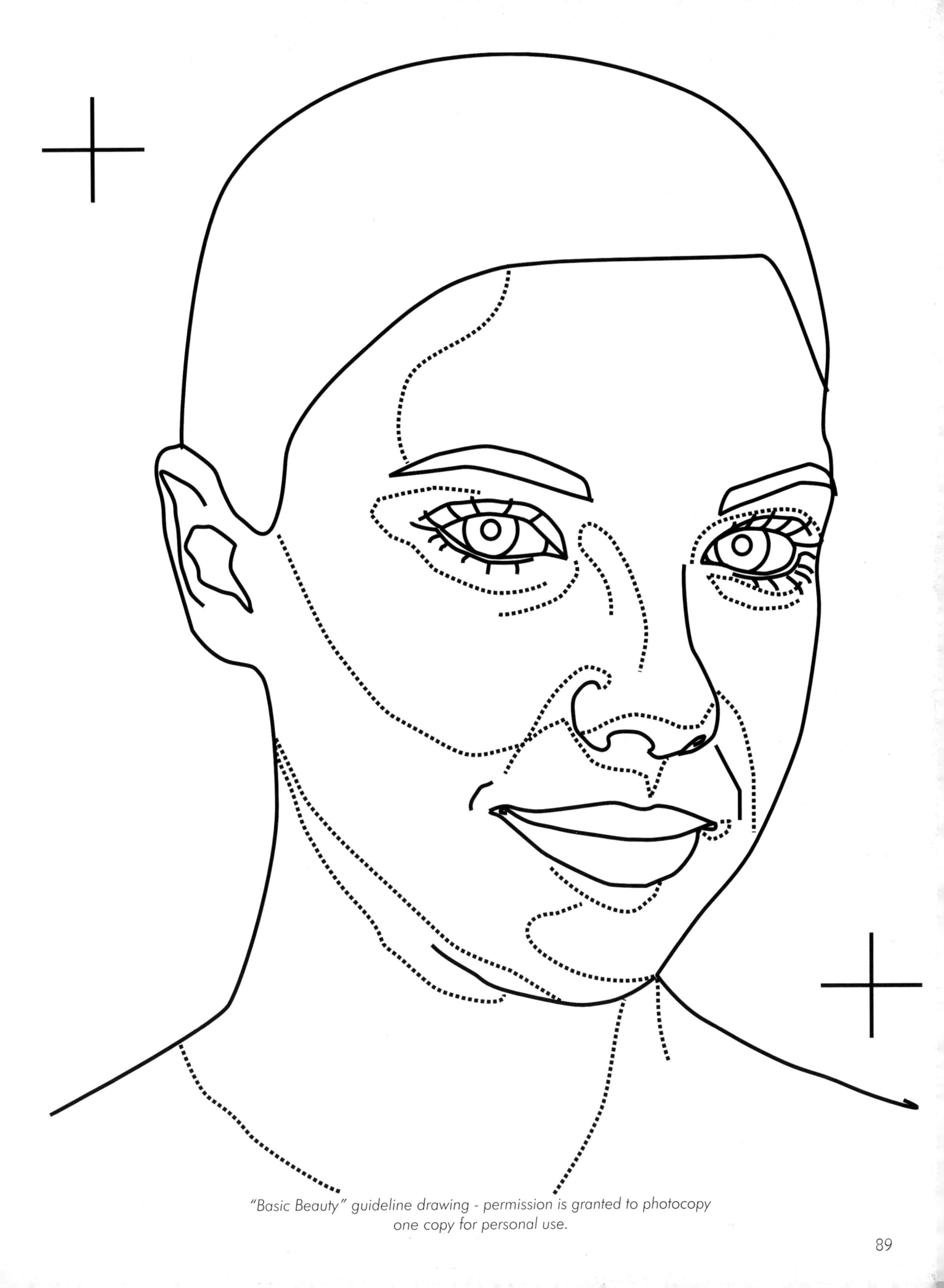

*"Basic Beauty" guideline drawing - permission is granted to photocopy one copy for personal use.*

A

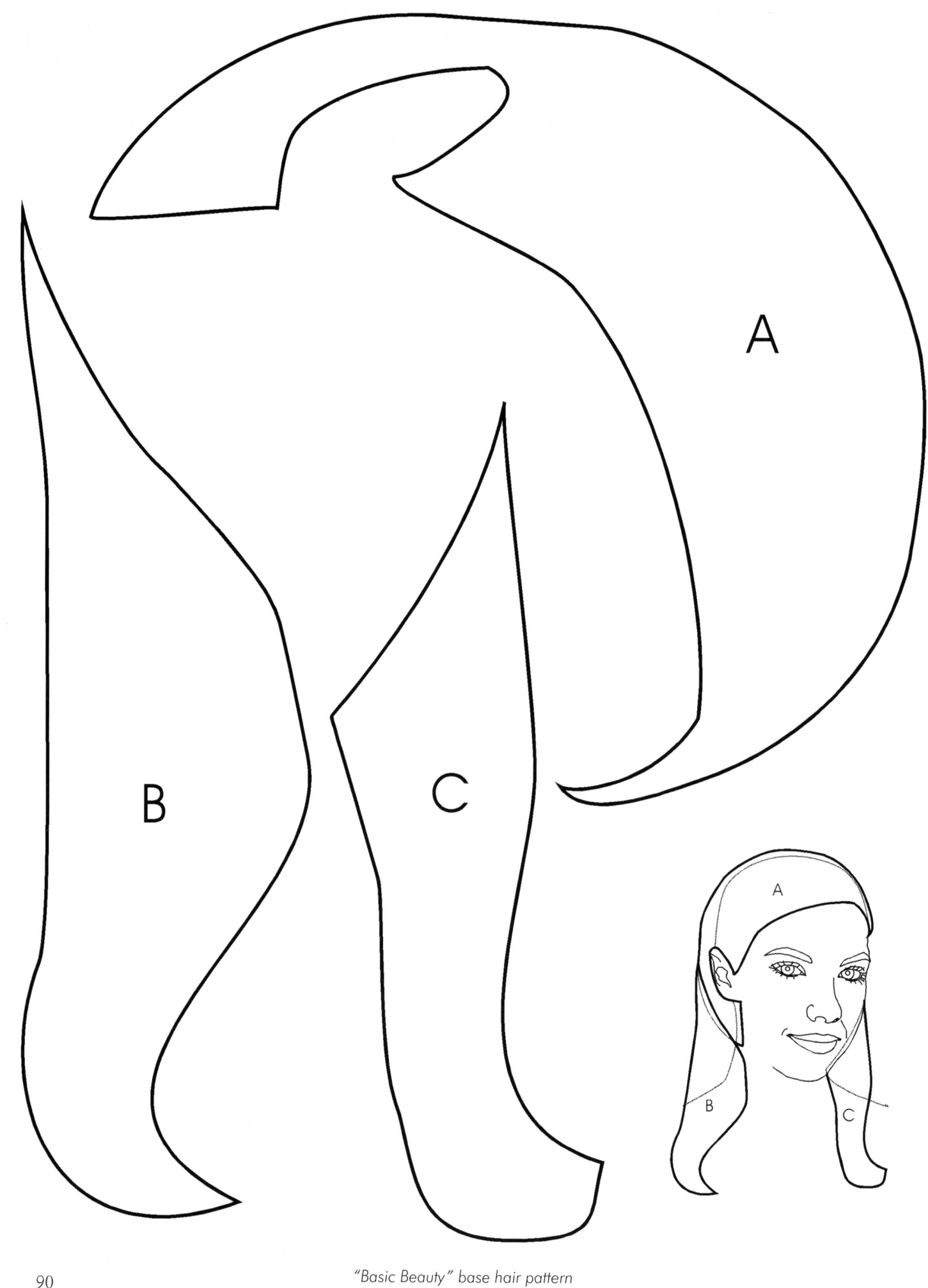

B     C

"Basic Beauty" base hair pattern

90

# SECTION V: Basic Steps and Patterns

## Quick Review

### Basic Step by Step Procedure
Now that you have experimented with the supplied face in the book, you are ready to paint someone else. Review the basic steps and have fun with it. You can do this!

### Basic Steps
Listed below are the basic steps that have been discussed in the previous sections.

1 Photograph your subject. (page 13)

2 Enlarge the photograph to the desired size.

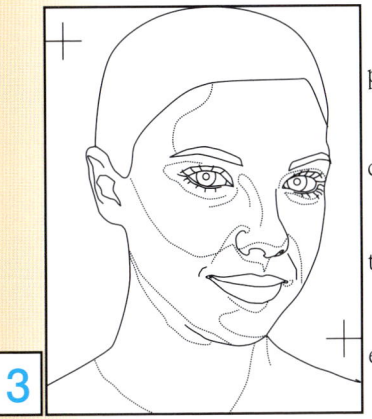

3 Create a guideline drawing from the photograph. (page 14)

4 Place the guideline drawing under the flesh colored fabric.

5 Paint the shading using the wet-on-wet technique. Iron dry. (page 16-21)

6 Paint the lips (page 23), nose (page 25), and eyes (page 27-30)

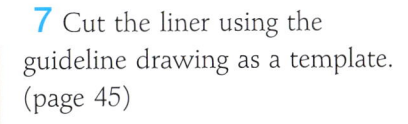

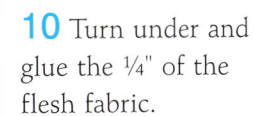

7 Cut the liner using the guideline drawing as a template. (page 45)

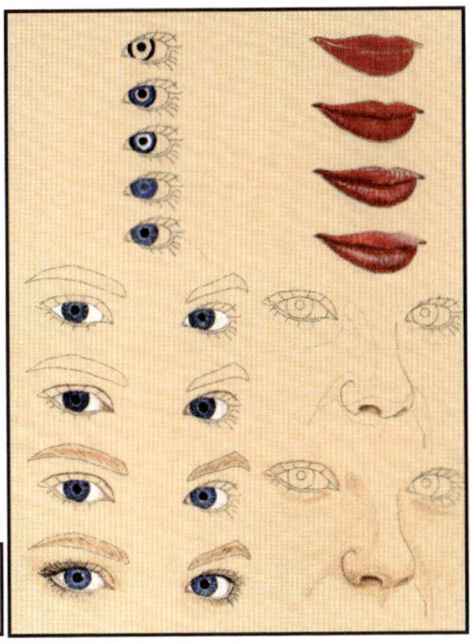

8 Fuse the liner to the back of the painted face.

9 Cut the flesh fabric ¼" beyond the liner.

10 Turn under and glue the ¼" of the flesh fabric.

11 Layer the background fabric on the firm tear away stabilizer. (page 45)

12 Position the painted face on the background fabric.

13 Create a pattern for clothing. (page 51)

14 Use the clothing pattern to cut the clothing.

15 Turn under the ¼" edge of the clothing.

91

**16** Lay the clothing over the painted face body.

**17** Create a template for the base hair. (page 57)

**18** Use the hair template to cut the base hair.

**19** Lay the base hair on the scull of the painted face.

**20** Add texture to the hair.

**21** Cover with a layer of tulle. (page 73)

**22** Pin the layers together.

**23** Stitch the layers together with invisible thread. (page 74).

**24** Cut away excess tulle. (page 75)

**25** Appliqué any turned under edges. (page 75)

**26** Tear away the stabilizer.

**27** Square up the background to the desired size.

**28** Add borders to the central design. (page 77)

**29** Layer the quilt top with the backing and batting.

**30** Baste the layers together.

**31** Quilt the layers. (page 83)

**32** Add embellishments to the design. (page 84)

**33** Square up the piece.

**34** Bind the quilt.

**35** Label the quilt. (page 86)

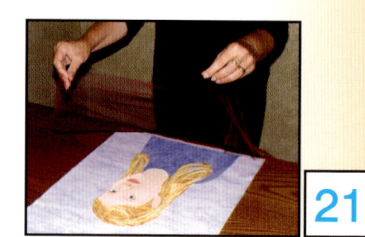

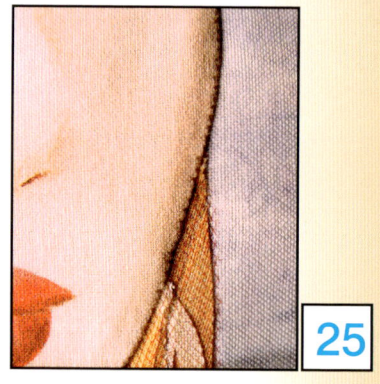

**Basic Beauty** by Bonnie Lyn McCaffery, Hawley, PA, 2002, 28" x 21". The face is Bonnie's daughter, Carly (McCaffery) Longhenry.

92

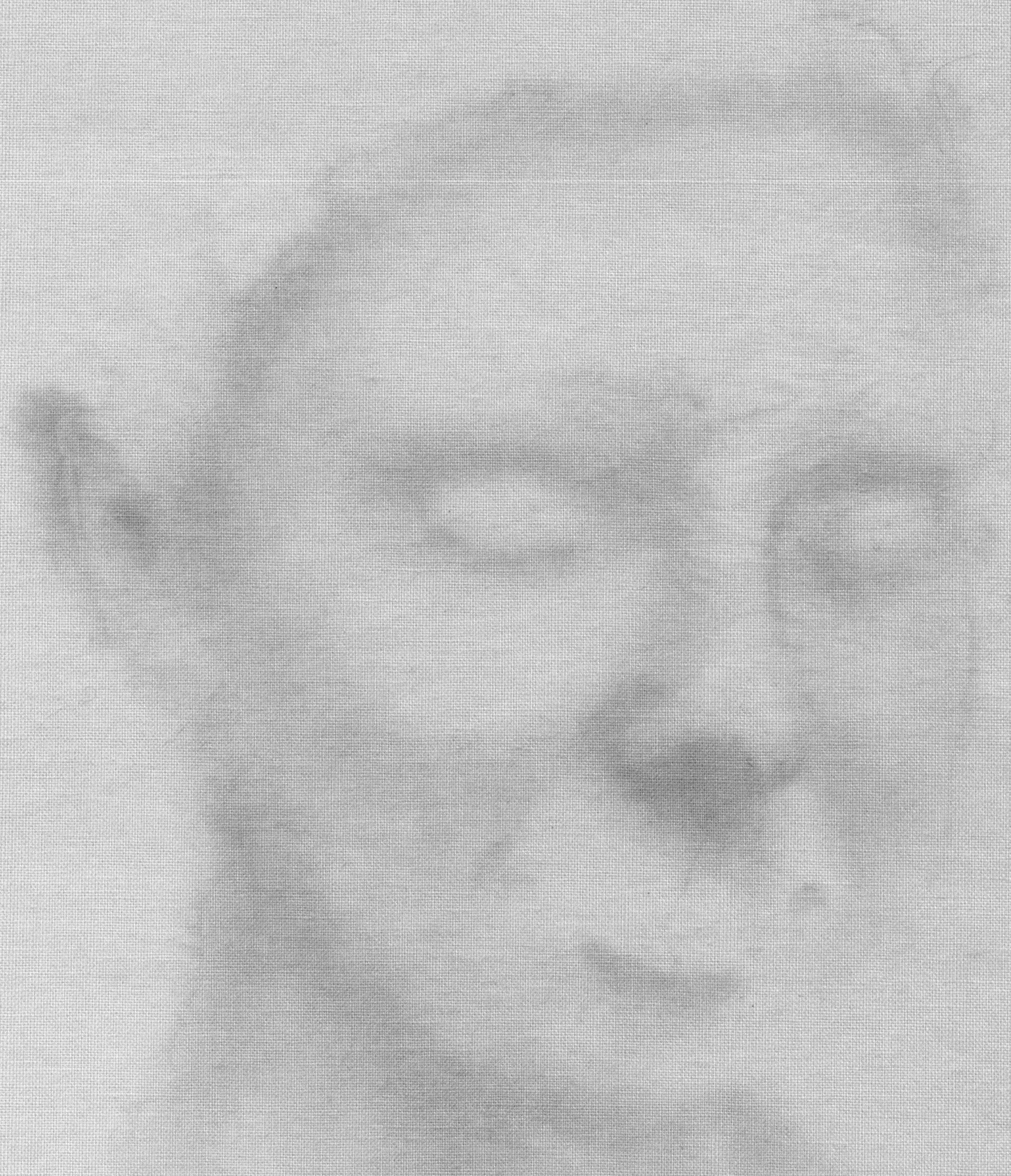

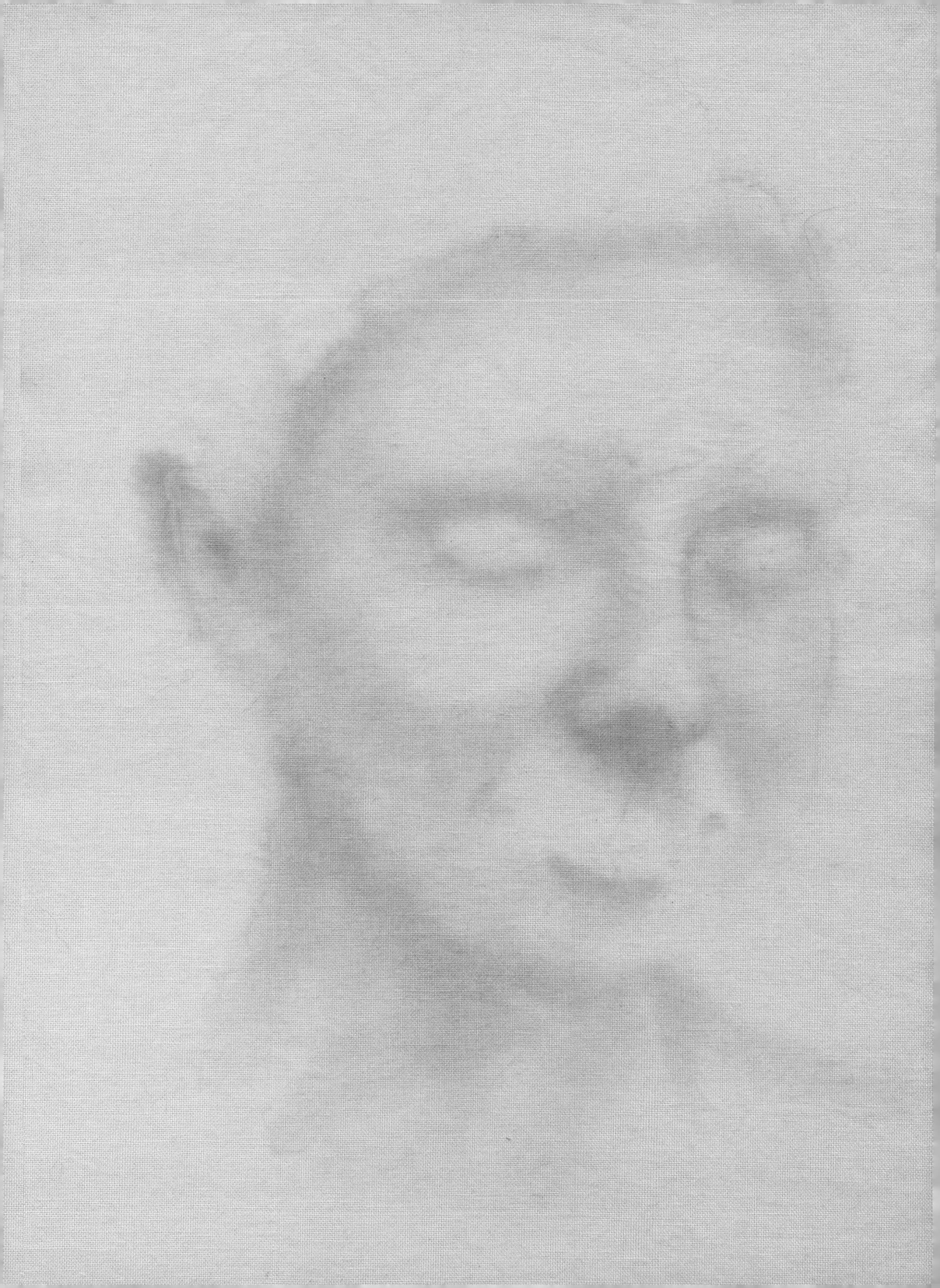

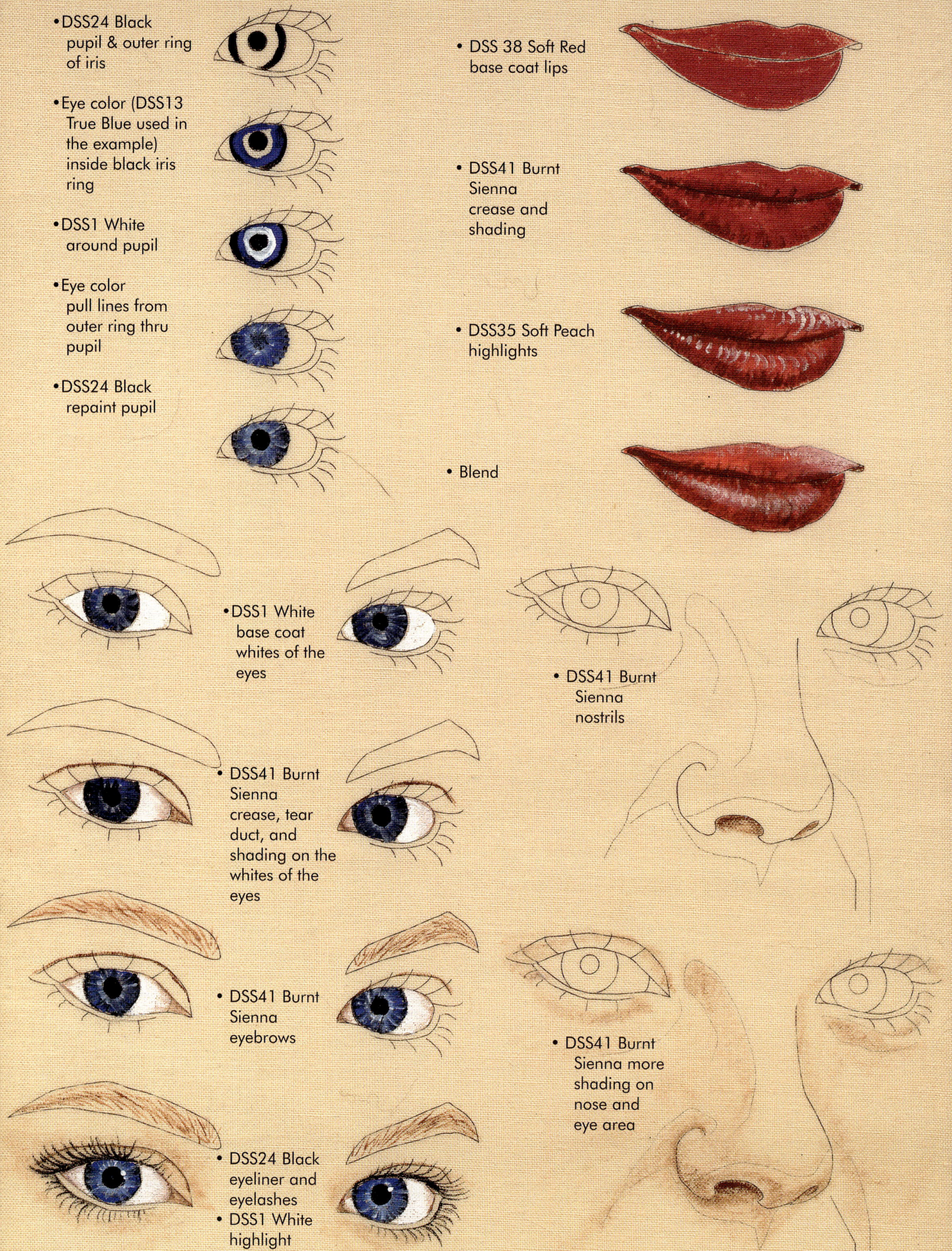

- DSS24 Black pupil & outer ring of iris

- Eye color (DSS13 True Blue used in the example) inside black iris ring

- DSS1 White around pupil

- Eye color pull lines from outer ring thru pupil

- DSS24 Black repaint pupil

- DSS 38 Soft Red base coat lips

- DSS41 Burnt Sienna crease and shading

- DSS35 Soft Peach highlights

- Blend

- DSS1 White base coat whites of the eyes

- DSS41 Burnt Sienna crease, tear duct, and shading on the whites of the eyes

- DSS41 Burnt Sienna eyebrows

- DSS24 Black eyeliner and eyelashes
- DSS1 White highlight

- DSS41 Burnt Sienna nostrils

- DSS41 Burnt Sienna more shading on nose and eye area

94  "Basic Beauty" feature reference

# Resources & Bibliography

## Bibliography

Andersen, Charlotte Warr. *Focus on Features.* Lafayette, CA: C & T Publishing, Inc., 1998.

Brystan, Lori. *High Impact Portrait Photography: Creative Techniques for Dramatic, Fashion-Inspired Portraits.* Buffalo, NY: Amherst Media, Inc., 2002.

Hammond, Lee. *How to Draw Lifelike Portraits from Photographs.* Cincinnati, OH: North Light Books, 1995.

Johnson, Vicki L. *Paint and Patches.* Paducah, KY: American Quilter's Society, 1995.

Madden, Angela. *Photo Fabrications: Easy Machine Appliqué from Family Photographs.* Harpenden, Herts, England: M.C.Q. Publications, 1999.

McCaffery, Bonnie Lyn. *Fantasy Fabrics: Techniques for Layered Surface Design.* Bothell, WA.: Martingale & Company, 1999.

McCaffery, Bonnie Lyn. *Fantasy Floral Quilts: Creating with Silk Flowers.* Bothell, WA: Martingale & Company, 2001.

## Resources

Bonnie Lyn McCaffery
HC-8 Box 8526
Hawley, PA 18428
bonnie@bonniemccaffery.com
http://BonnieMcCaffery.com
Flesh colored fabric, DecoArt SoSoft Fabric Paints, brushes, Tintzl, books and more. Lecture and workshop information available upon request.

eQuilter.com
http://equilter.com/
Toll Free: 1 - 877 - FABRIC -3
Local:   303-527-0856
Boulder, CO  80301

# About the Author

Bonnie Lyn McCaffery lives in Hawley, Pennsylvania with her husband, Michael, their golden retriever, and several cats. Their three daughters, Heather, Carly, and Abby, are now grown and off on their own. In their spare time, Bonnie and Michael enjoy just sitting on the deck and enjoying the fresh mountain air.

In 1998, Bonnie was awarded the Jewel Pearce Patterson Scholarship that sent her to Innsbruck, Austria to attend the European Quilt Market and the International Quilt Expo. This whet her appetite to international travel. Since then she has taught in England, Ireland, Scotland, France, Sweden, Denmark, Canada, and Curaçao as well as within the United States.

She has been published in a wide variety of magazines including *American Quilter's Society Magazine, Art Quilt Magazine, Craftworks, McCall's Quilting, Popular Patchwork, Magic Patch, Quilting Arts Magazine,* and *Quilting International*. Bonnie has appeared twice on *Simply Quilts* - once demonstrating how to create Fantasy Fabric and a second time demonstrating Portrait Quilts.

Bonnie specializes in experimenting with new techniques in quilting and making them easy for everyone to do. Foundation pieced kaleidoscope quilts, free-form appliqué, dimensional quilts, hand painted fabric, fantasy fabrics, as well as painting faces on fabric are a few of the techniques she has explored.

*Fantasy Fabrics: Techniques for Layered Surface Design* was her first book. This technique is for creating a new fabric by capturing a variety of different items (cut fabric, ribbon, thread, Tintzl, metallic stars, artificial flowers and lots more) under a sheer top layer of tulle.

Her second book, *Fantasy Floral Quilts: Creating with Silk Flowers* explored many different types of quilts that can be created by capturing artificial flowers under a layer of sheer tulle – bouquets, wreaths, album style, floral embellished pieced quilts, landscapes, and many more.